$$1 + 1 = 2$$

TWO SANE

A psychological documentation through poetic and artistic memoirs that revealed to the author that his entries were just two different personalities of himself that were trying to communicate with each other to make them both self-aware of the duality their own separate existences. This collection of material was written in a scattered chaos of pieces that were in a non-sequitur order. Each piece was artistically fueled by raw undeniable emotions, they were sourced by a high intelligence and perception, and they were later organized into chapters for the reader.

This book goes through the thoughts of someone with Dissociative Identity Disorder, which contains a universal range of subject matter including humans, love, society, drugs, earth, government, spirit, art, creation, psychology, and self. This book helped the author find out who he really was, has helped blast informational light to countless people that read it understand themselves better, the disorder better, and the combined sum of these moments we call our life better. When one is able to understand an abnormality that is the very action that defines what we all consider normal.

FROM THE AUTHOR(S)

Dear Readers,

I am a completely different being than who I was when I wrote my first book, "Walking the Line." If anything, that book was nothing more than a philosophical mental excavation in search of who I really was. Every time I would look in a mirror, all I would see was this organism staring back at me, its eyes were shifting side-to-side as they dilated. It was almost as if another entity was examining what I was looking at it, and that feeling alone gave me nothing but inner torment. What am I? I did everything I possibly could to figure out who I was. I smoked marijuana for ten years, with each hit I thought I was expanding my ability to become more self-aware, but in reality, I was only escaping my true reality in a fog of smoke.

I consumed psychedelic mushrooms to alter my mindset, and even then, I would only partially have moments of realization that I would soon forget once the hallucinations had ended. I did stints of snorting cocaine, and the chemical rush of the dopamine allowed me to feel out the true sensations that I was unable to normally enjoy because I had been so disassociated from myself. Then came the momentary stretch where I pushed the limits of my reality and sanity with LSD. My brain was able to tap into some sort of universal consciousness that vibrated throughout the galaxy, and yet, despite having the knowledge of the cosmos stored into my subconscious, I was still unable to put together the two puzzle pieces that comprised me.

I was in tremendous emotional pain. When you are nothing more than an ever-changing entity who surfs through society to find another version of yourself, all you want to be is like everyone else; a plastic shape that fits in with the masses. When the emotional pain became too great, the only drug that seemed to fix the broken shape-shifting machine that I was were opiates. I started off small with the basic opioid-based narcotics that would be given to a child with a toothache, after building six years of a tremendous tolerance and habit; by the end, I was on something eight times more powerful than morphine, and I was inhaling faster than doctors could prescribe it. I tried committing suicide six times; with each time there was a learning curve. By the last suicide attempt I actually felt death; miraculously, my internal resilience made me cling to the light of life. walked away a stronger, more-driven man, and one with a mind that was a tactical, ever-changing lock that could not be solved or broken.

I went to five different psychiatrists, as I fearlessly displayed psychological conditions in a continuous fashion, so that these doctors would intentionally believe my conscious manipulation of their diagnosis of me, and all because I wanted a label and medication to describe and help me cope with what I was. I accepted the diagnosis of ADD. After the stimulants failed to fix the problem, I accepted the diagnosis of Bipolar. After the mood stabilizers did not fix my internal pain, I accepted the diagnosis of Schizoaffective. And when the anti-psychotics did not help after two years; I finally just accepted I was forever broken and I quit looking for who I was and started writing. In the first book, one could see hints of confusion as to who I really was. I had even taken on the diagnosis of Dissociative Identity Disorder, because I noticed how, under extreme stressful situations that were mostly brought out by my parents, I would just have the ability to hide inside my brain and feel nothing. That was all my consciousness could do to cope – vanish.

After reviewing my first book once it was published, I started to notice that I seemed to be talking to myself; or rather, another version of me was talking to myself. That's when I realized that the first book, although I deemed it worthy of being called finished, was, in fact, not finished at all. It was just the beginning of me finding out who we really were. As an artist, I tried to write all of my thoughts in a beautiful, aesthetic manner, which made the process of this true self-discovery not only a magnificent thing to read, but it was beautiful thing to accept about who or what I really was. We were two men sharing one brain: a small, scared child who needed to constantly be taken care of, and a twenty-nine-year-old man who had to observe all of his behavior and eventually come to his own rescue every time he made a bad conscious choice in life.

   We were nothing more than a reflection of other people whom we consciously deemed worthy of impersonation: a reflection of a reflection, and, in reality, we were no one at all. This book is the psychological documentation of two conscious entities accepting what we really were, when everyone all around us could see – plain as day – how we were two different people. How do you tell someone you love that he is cognitively split into two pieces so he actually accepts it? This psychological documentation was posted as it was written, day-by-day, to everyone on a social network. Not only did they watch me slowly accept what I was, but we both accepted who we were. This book has not only shed light on hundreds of people who were trapped in the mental fog also, but it allowed everyone who read it to finally understand those rare people whom they knew in life, and why they were so drastically different. This is my gift to myself, and it is my gift to the world: "Two Sane."

Let the trauma slowly heal; live life with an undying zeal.

Empathically,

Zachary Philip Freeman

TWO
SANE

Written By:

Zachary Philip Freeman (A)

Zachary Philip Freeman (B)

Edited By:

Tony Eichberger

Special Thanks:

Mary Kay Delost

Jaclyn Godfrey

Logan Kelly

Reid Simon

A metamorphosis from me into we

When the Alpha created the Omega

Defensive variables were generated offensively

Needing the control in complete chaos

From A spawned B

Aα

Magnetic Man

One can pick him out of a crowd, his thoughts are unique and intelligent, his actions are swift and quiet; but that makes what he does extremely loud. He doesn't look like the rest, he follows his own path of style, and when you approach him, the words he speaks to you are a verbal test. The level on which he engages you seems so rational and sane, little do you know he is only a reflection of your personality, he is psychologically wording what you inherently wish to hear, which makes you see yourself in him, and this sensation is anything but inane.

His presence is like looking into a spiritual soul mirror, everything that comes out of his mouth is so wise, and those thoughts only help you see who you really are much clearer. He is like a drug that opens your eyes, you can't seem to get enough of him, and he is filled with pure truth; none of the usual lies. You instantly want to be friends, you only want the best, you want him in your social circle, you feel he brings out a better you; he is not like the rest. You desire his presence in your group, you want him to join your pack, just wait until he meets the rest of the guys, they won't believe what you have found, and until they meet him they will just think he is just a myth; you may see his front, but he has no back.

You exchange information, you make plans to meet, for some reason you can never seem to catch him, because he seems to keep really odd hours; a constant transformation. When you do eventually rally, he seems slightly different than the last time you met, that's because he is trying to keep continuity with whom you expect to see, and he won't reveal who he really is; that is for the finale. The reality of the situation is that he is more than just one person, he is too many people to put a number on, one day he is a psychological mastermind, and the next day he is just a husk of a person; that hero who magnetized you is simply gone.

He morphs into the person he needs to reflect, he can be nearly anyone he wants to be, you know there is something unique about him, but it's nearly impossible for you to detect. He has countless voices that depending on the situation will change vocal tone, he avoids societal interaction because he hates wearing a mask, his true nature only comes out when he can be in the privacy of his domain; when he is finally alone. He is a human twenty-sided dice, you will never know the outcome, and he's grown so good at acting; you will never know where his intentions will come from.

The majority would fear him because humans fear the

unknown, and if you only knew all the lives he has lived; your mind

would truly be blown. He is a rarity of the human race, so most

people who live in his situation prefer to stay in the darkness and in

their own place. Everyone he meets, if his consciousness deems his

or her actions worthy, he will often mimic and repeat. He's the

chameleon who no one understands, he is the oddity that people love

to have around, but because of his lifestyle, he doesn't want to be

found; he is the magnetic man...

I AM A COLLECTION OF A COLLECTION

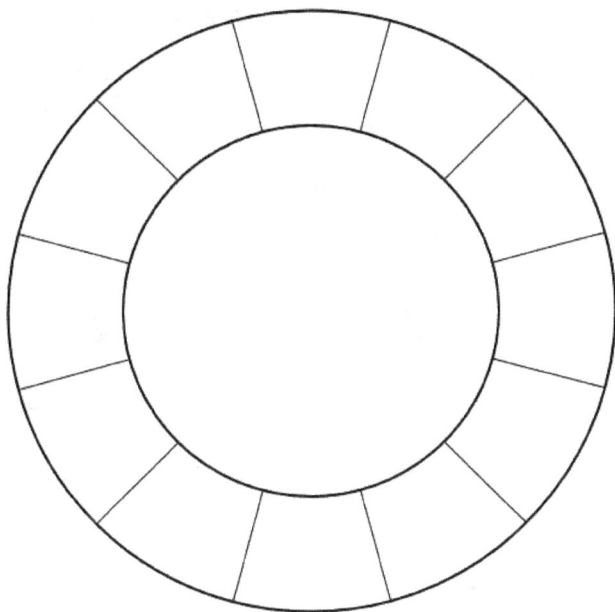

I AM NOTING AND EVERYTHING AT ONCE

The Six Chapters of Self-Examination

One

MACHINES AWAKE IN THE HUSKS OF WEAKER MEN WHO PREVIOUSLY EXISTED THE PAST

DAY, AND THEY WILL HAVE TO BREAK THE MOLD THAT WAS FORMED WITHOUT DISMAY;

NO CONCERNS OF EMOTION OR WHAT THE REST OF HUMANITY WILL GO ON TO SAY...

Two

WHEN ONE'S PRIORITIES ARE WAKING UP TO KILL MORE CREATURES THAN THEY SAVE,

ABSORBING MORE INTELIGENCE THROUGH PLEASURE THAN PHYSICAL DRIVE ON EVERY

THOUGHT WAVE, AND LYING TO THOSE who ONLY NEED TO HEAR THE TRUTH THAT THEY

CRAVE; THIS ONLY SPEAKS IN VOLUMES ABOUT THE FUTURE THAT THESE REPEATED

ACTIONS WILL PAVE...

Three

LANDS OF CONSUMERISM DICTATE YOUR ASSOCIATIONS WITHIN THREE CLASSES, BECAUSE

ETHNICITY IS SIMILARLY A SHROUD THAT NOTIONS STATISTICAL PERCEPTIONS OF YOUR

EXISTENCE TO THE MASSES; A PYRAMID-LIKE SYSTEM THAT THOSE DEEMED WORTHY GET

THE GREENER GRASSES

Four

"IN ALL SPIRITUALITIES THAT RISE, WHETHER A PRIEST OF THE CLOTH OR SHAMAN OF THE SKIES, BECAUSE THERE IS NO DENYING THE ENERGY IN OUR CRIES; THOSE DEVISE TO USE IT AS A DISGUISE TO THOSE WHO IT SUPPLIES..."

Five

THE ARTIST CAN ENDLESSLY VERBALIZE A CONTINUOUS FLOW OF NEW IDEAS THAT ARE THE NEXT OF THE GRANDIOSE VISIONS; YET, THEY HAVE THE INABILITY TO GENERATE A PRODUCT BECAUSE THEY ARE LACKING IN MOTIVATIONS; TO BE DOOMED WITHOUT ANY OF THE EXECUTIVE DECISIONS...

Six

NOTIONS OF THOSE WHO DESIRE TO END PSYCHOLOGICAL PROBLEMS IN ENDLESS DEVOTIONS; YET, THE LABELS THAT ARE GIVEN RESULT IN OVERMEDICATED, FLATTENED EMOTIONS; THE WEARY SOCIETAL COMMOTIONS...

"He says 1. She says 0. He says 1. She says 0. He says 1. She says 0. Then they both stand back and look at their conversation. "It's like we were almost human."

"Constitution is a meal ticket to perception."

"Personality is intelligence displayed through charisma."

ONE

MACHINES AWAKE IN THE HUSKS OF WEAKER MEN WHO PREVIOUSLY EXISTED THE PAST DAY, AND THEY MUST BREAK THE MOLD THAT WAS PREVIOUSLY FORMED WITHOUT DISMAY; NO CONCERNS OF EMOTION OR WHAT THE REST OF HUMANITY WILL GO ON TO SAY...

"Don't you stop the love, because the love might just stop you."

"Fear prevents psychological deviation; until the stagnation of self preservation becomes a conscious issue of one's hesitation."

"Nothing can be lost that time cannot cure; find the cure in lost time."

HUMANITY

Hardly Human

We are nothing more than a complex organic machine, from the nutrients that power us in every cuisine, from the liquids that sustain us from our canteen, and every daily task that keeps us on a routine. When we sleep at night it gives us energy to burn in the day, we wake up on a schedule to work for pay, and we do this systematically; we always obey. Our blood is the life force that is our oil, we maintain a constant body temperature so we do not spoil, and our muscles absorb shock so we can recoil. Our organs are components that keep us alive, our computer-like brain that makes us strive, and we keep reproducing because of our sex drive.

Our combined population is a mechanical social organization, everyone has a daily job that is done on rotation, and we work as hard as we can until we get a vacation; comply or face starvation. It does not matter your color or model of human building block, no matter the language that is spoken when you talk, because you will still just be another member of the flock. The police are designed to take malfunctioning units away, our doctors try to give us health everyday, and our priests try to keep us from going morally astray. The schools are deigned to program the masses, the teachers give us structure in all of our classes, and it is all designed to keep order;

with or without the rose-tinted glasses.

The lawyers enforce the laws that the politicians made code, we follow the rules because it is our operational mode, and the daily progress will never be slowed; instead, it has been bestowed. The military ensures that every government is in order, soldiers make sure that territories obey their border, and with tremendous firepower there will be no disorder. When the cogs vote a faction to be elected and the loser will cower, that is when the chosen one will control the next superpower, because someone has to dictate orders from the tower. Bigger machines need to control smaller machines, just as the spread of disease is dictated by the quality of our vaccines, and how our health ensues due to the quality of our genes.

There is one thing that keeps everything calculated, it is the most important machine that can never be dated, and it is invisible and cannot be debated. The thing that keeps everything moving is consumerism in a capitalistic society, it is the source of everyone's anxiety, it is why we lose our sobriety, and it is what gives us such global notoriety. It's the products that we will always desire, the marketing department turns a frugal man into a buyer, and it's why most of us will never retire; the next status symbol that we must acquire. We are hardly human and these are the reasons why, these are the mechanics that make us comply, and these are the very things that make us robots that will not die.

Following Followers

People who are lost tend to seek out people who can lead. Leaders tend to seek out people who are lost. We are attracted to those who can illustrate power, because we want to learn how to be powerful ourselves. When you are powerless, you always seek out someone who can help you learn to lead; and when you have power, you always seek out those who want to follow. It's the natural process of being a human. Only those with inner strength can lead, while those who have inner weakness will always follow.

Identifying Ignorance

The deaf cannot hear. The blind cannot see. The ignorant cannot think. When you cannot hear, the better you can see. When you cannot see, the better you can hear. When you are ignorant, you refuse to learn – because you are content with the way you think. Being content with the way you think is like being blind, deaf, and ignorant at the same time. When you are constantly evolving it does not matter if you are deaf and blind, because you may be stuck with a cane or reading Braille, but the mind always has the ability to evolve depending on the circumstances.

Reluctant Routine

You are stuck in a routine that makes you less human and more of a machine. Everyday you repeat the same tasks; you are afraid to break free and take off your daily mask. The only thing that keeps you from rebelling is your minimal reward band, when in reality the power is all in your hand. If you could only feel the rage inside you that makes you tired of this societal game; if you could only be the match that ignites an internal flame.

The reality is you can do anything you desire; you can break free from this control if you feel your inner fire. The trick is to not listen to anyone but your inner voice; you can break your shackles once you realize it is all your choice. The nine-to-five is slowly killing you, as all you do is collect material possessions; your biggest problem is you ask no questions. Everything is built like this to control the masses – and you are a fool if you follow all the millions of jackasses.

The one emotion you need to set you free is small doses of rage that will help you see. Only the brave walk in a different direction from the flock; when you start to defy the masses, you will be in for a shock. People will follow you instead of giving you resistance; they will admire your will and only give you assistance. The next time you are put in a position where you can't stand it anymore, free yourself and walk right out that door.

Terminating Terms

Everyone commands: they shout, they dictate, they force you to comply, and no power is ever in your hands. The only power that you do have is not even really yours, for they are things you are forced to do on a daily basis – because they are your list of chores. After you go to college, after you get your job, after you meet your spouse, after you have your kids, and after they grow up – you suddenly get the first taste of freedom.

You can do things you actually want to do, not what is shoved by society down your throat; your mood will jump to happy from when it was once blue. Finally, for once in your lifetime, you can do what you desire, and it is this time in your life when the stagnant waters dry up and something lights your internal fire.

Limiting Limitations

When the sky is the limit, you only limit yourself to how high the sky can get. Try not to set limits; be someone who is unlimited in what one can do; you can accomplish anything you put your mind to. Don't corner yourself in a label, psychologically isolating yourself from your full potential. Instead, label things you want to do; if you work hard enough at it, you will succeed at whatever you hope to accomplish. Human beings are limitless by nature; so don't let your limits squash your potential, because we become anything we want at any time we want. Adopting this psychological notion will help you escape your limits, and then you can truly become something that is limitless in nature.

Wise Wisdom

True wisdom comes from those who have lived many lives within their lifetimes. Since we are forms of organic intelligence, we learn from trial and error. The man who walks down many roads will make many mistakes; but with each mistake, he learns what not to do. Just because someone has a high intelligence level does not make them immune from error. It takes wisdom to understand how your intelligence may lead you to make an ignorant decision, and it takes intelligence to understand how your attained wisdom will strengthen your ability to make the proper choices in life. Many intelligent people can make really stupid mistakes – but it's recognizing those mistakes that will make you truly wise.

Structured Strength

A slight amount of brain damage can actually be good for an individual, because what clouds your judgment one day will open your eyes the next. The trick is finding the right amount of brain damage that will hurt you just enough to only make you stronger. If you overdo it, you could be lost forever; but if you find the right balance, you will be forever grateful. It's a very thin line between brilliance and insanity; the trick is walking the line and balancing on that tightrope. If you fall, you will end up worse off than you were before; but if you successfully balance yourself, you will be the cream that rises to the top – and you can see reality for what it really is.

Fickle Fancier

When you find something special, something unique, and something amazing, you become infatuated with it because it's like nothing you have ever seen before. You begin to crave it, obsess over it, and you become infatuated with it. With each passing day, you cherish what you have found; it is your new favorite thing. The more you look at it, observe it, and cherish it; day-by-day, the novelty slowly wears off. Eventually, as time goes on, you become more and more desensitized to your greatest object of your desire; you glorified it for too long and with too much zeal.

Eventually, your treasure becomes something too familiar to you, and you lose interest in what you thought was so great about it in the first place. After a period of time, you will begin to find that what you once loved so dearly is now something that is getting old to look at. You no longer see what's special about your prize, and it becomes clutter within your life. Soon after your infatuation is over, you start to notice little defects in something you once loved so dearly. With each passing day, you criticize it more and more from every angle. The fascination you once had with it suddenly becomes a moot part of your life. As time continues, all you can see are the object's flaws, rather than what made it once so special.

Then you reach a point where that thing no longer gives you passion; rather, a feeling of distaste and disgust, because the flaws jump out at you – and what you once saw as beauty has long since faded. You start to develop a loathing for that object, as you move it to a place where you can't see it as often; you don't want to be reminded of the beauty you once saw in it. Time passes, and even the occasions when you randomly stumble upon it still trigger that negative stigma; you wish you wouldn't have seen it in the first place. You then hide it in a clandestine spot somewhere, where you know you will never see it on a frequent basis.

As time passes, you forget about that thing you once cherished, so you move on to find something new that will suit your fancy and interest. Years will pass until the one day when you are doing some housecleaning, and then, to your surprise, you find that one object you had once embraced so dearly. Looking at it again with fresh eyes, you see everything you once saw to be great in that object – and you fall in love with it all over again.

You look past those flaws you once saw, as you can only see the beauty you hold in your hands. This is the cycle of everything you have once owned, and now you realize that you must cherish things in small doses if you want to keep them in your limelight. What is special one day will become garbage the next – until you don't see it for awhile, and then, it once again becomes your greatest asset.

Critical Crisis

Going into a mode of crisis is the best opportunity we can experience. In a mode of crisis, everything is expendable; when we feel that things are going fine, nothing is expendable. You need to sometimes realize what you are willing to give up in life, before you can get what you really need. We become so attached to people, places, and things that we are afraid to let anything go. We fear change, and, a majority of time, we can only truly change when everything goes wrong.

When crisis strikes, you are forced to pick what goes or what stays; before we go through crisis, we are only living to play. Crisis is critical to your emotional, physical, and psychological development; so the next time you are forced into a corner, just make sure to have your wits about you so you can choose the best way to manipulate your environment for success. The thing to remember about environmental manipulation is that, a majority of the time, you are merely manipulating yourself.

That could be a problem – or that could very well be your solution. Just think ahead and choose whether you are manipulating yourself for your betterment or for your destruction, because sometimes manipulation requires effort from both sides. Just as the Chinese view it, crisis is opportunity knocking – whether you can hear the knock, that is all up to your perception to choose.

Fighter's Flight

If you want to find out what you are truly capable of, put yourself in a position where you are trapped and need to escape. Your brain will come up with every possible logical solution. You will be triggered into a mode of both fight and flight at the same time, as you desperately will do anything to survive. You will first call your family; if you receive no help from them, then you will call your closest friends who truly understand you.

If that doesn't work, then you will start to reach out to people you haven't talked to in years – people who have been watching you struggle throughout your entire life; people who have been sitting on the sidelines, watching you evolve through your struggles. And, believe it or not, one of these people will be kind enough to save your life.

When people watch your struggles, appreciate your brilliance, love your creativity – you have been unknowingly contributing to their lives the whole time you have lived yours, and, to them, money is no matter. I know the media portrays nothing but the horrors of society, but you have to know in your heart that there are good people out there, and those good people will eventually reveal themselves and rescue you from suffering. Putting yourself in that need to escape will show you not only what you are capable of doing, but it will also show you who your biggest supporters are.

Controlled Chaos

In a world dictated by complete chaos, we spend so much time trying to control the chaos that the control begins to become chaotic itself. That's why people rebel and deviate from the norm – because they are tired of being controlled, and, deep down in our hearts, we yearn for that instinctual freedom we once had from the beginning of our humanity.

When you openly embrace the chaos that comes from within you, your real personality will start to blossom. So many people spend their entire lives being controlled by other individuals that it isn't until much later in life when they finally snap and say, "No! This is what I am going to do, for once!" After you embrace chaos and let it flow through the core of your essence, you will not only find the unknown beautiful but the chaos will provide you with life experiences you never imagined possible. You will meet new people, you will do things you never conceived of, and you will discover how incredible pandemonium can be.

We will never experience what it feels like to truly be alive until we give up the control that dictates our daily behavior and start comprehending what an unrestrained lifestyle presents us with.

There is a trick to chaos – having controlled chaos. Being conscious enough to know when to deviate, and, at the same time, knowing when to hold yourself back; controlled chaos. Controlled chaos is a skill, and the way to hone that skill is by using something we, as human beings, repress on a day-to-day basis, which is called instinct.

Doing something instinctually is something that is beaten out of us at an early age. The Powers That Be don't want you to be instinctual because that poses a threat to the control that has been established over the past 8,000 years. It took a great while to set up the control structure that exists, and that's why people reprimand you when you act chaotic. The trick to reviving your instincts is to try small doses of chaos per day. Get in your car and let your instincts drive you to your destination.

Explore, find something new, go somewhere you haven't been – or better yet, go to someplace you have journeyed to for quite awhile, and deviate from what you would normally do. You will be more than pleased with your outcome. We are billions of beings running around doing the same daily tasks, for our same daily jobs, for our same daily people – and you shouldn't be afraid to do something you would not normally do. Nearly everything that I love in my life I found through chaotic events; this includes people, places, or things. Don't fear the unknown – embrace it! Why not be like the chemicals in nearly every organism that exists on this planet?

Bounce around until you find a receptor that you are happy with, acknowledge it exists, remember where it is, and continue along with your life. What do you think causes depression? Answer: a lack of chaos. What do you think causes frustration, anger, and rage? Answer: too much control. What will give you your freedom to do anything in this world? Answer: controlled chaos.

Absorbing Acceptance

When you accept who someone is, deep down inside you are actually accepting who you really are. We all contain the same drives, insecurities, emotions, and desires that drive our actions on a day-to-day basis. We are all just products of the lives we have lived, and the best thing you can do for yourself is realize that we are all experiencing the same problems – just at different times in our life. So, if you meet someone whose problem has such a negative stigma it makes you want to distance yourself from them – just remember, in the back of your mind, how you could have possibly been that person if you had lived their life in their set of circumstances. Most of all, you could quite possibly become that person later on in your life.

You should feel empathy for every individual, because you don't know what he or she went through that led him or her toward the choices he or she has made. If you end up trapped in the same situation as them, you will only empathize later on; you will realize you could have stopped making the choices that brought you to that place if you only would have accepted them from the beginning. You would have known what actions to avoid so you wouldn't end up in the same situation.

LOVE

Passionate Pain

Everything beautiful on this Earth has a self-defense mechanism to keep others away from it. You can view it in two ways: take the pain to enjoy the beauty, or take the beauty and enjoy the pain. Beauty always comes with a price, because the most beautiful things in this world need to be protected; otherwise, everyone would take the beauty for himself or herself, and there would be no beauty left for the rest of us. If you truly want the beauty, you must accept the pain that comes with it.

Passionate Passions

You understand the core of me; with your love my eyes can focus, and I can see. I may be well-traveled, but my experiences don't help me when I become unraveled. You want to escape your environment, and I want to do the same; the only thing that saves me is when I say, in my head, your name. You accept who I am – you pried open my shell and took a look inside of the clam. Your capacity to love is limitless – and because of that, I want to make you my princess. Most would view this as infatuation, but they are too blind to see how we are each other's salvation. Together we will solve all of our ailments; we will prevent each other's derailments. The feelings I have for you are not just some fleeting mood; they are truly something imbued.

Angst Again

You just met her, and she is constantly on your mind; she has made such an impression on you that you feel this is a once-in-a-lifetime find. When she is off doing her own thing, just as people have to do, you wonder if she's thinking of you. When you are sexually attracted, intellectually attracted, you think on the same waves; she is on your mind so often it leaves you distracted.

When you are with her, even though it is from a great distance; you only see her words on a screen, but she does not fail to permeate every core of your existence. You haven't even thought about sex with her, because that's not what this connection is about – it is about sharing moments and thoughts that happen so fast they're a blur. You dream of the day when you will finally see her face-to-face; you will uncontrollably run to her, grab her with all of your might, hold her close as possible, kiss that amazing soul, and praise that you are for once in the same place.

Distance only makes your yearning deeper; she builds your emotions so high, you know with every rational thought that she is a keeper. She heightens every emotion you feel, gives you strength when you are weak, and every word she says renews your zeal. For so long life felt so distant from your disassociated eyes, everything was unreal; you operated as an empty husk, but now you have met the perfect woman, and all these symptoms she does nothing but heal. Just a week ago, you felt like ending it all; but now you have found an essence that strengthens you and makes you stand tall. Flawless in every way, you can't pick out a single problem with whom she is; this astounds you because, because no one was ever perfect enough for a man to call his.

As she goes about her daily routine, minutes turn to hours, hours turn to days, and you can't wait until she returns to brighten your day. It is painful being so distant for someone you view as nothing but great; but for now, you will just have to suffer the lover's angst – until she returns at a later date.

Beautiful Brain

From the moment you saw her picture you were entranced with her lovely face, and she gravitated towards you from your words that you put out in cyberspace. You messaged her to get to know the woman behind the beauty, after conversing with her you found out that you have things in common, even after barley knowing her she makes you feel amazing, and even with the combination of intelligence and grace she does not present an attitude that she is snooty. Personal information was exchanged and now you have a way to message her anytime you want, then the next day you have retrograde amnesia of everything that had transpired between the two of you, you are sick in the head, and you don't want this treasure to know something that really isn't you, so you send her a message revealing your whole situation, because to this woman you don't want to maintain a constant front.

Days go by after revealing who you really are, you see her log online, but the fear that is inside you makes you not want to contact her, so you stay distant and far. Finally you can't hold back your feelings for this woman who has just recently captivated your heart, you bravely message her with a passive statement asking her how she is doing, you want to communicate with her so badly, but the paranoia and fear keeps you apart. A day later you receive a message back from her, she doesn't appear to be distant, which you find rather shocking; she knows everything about you and she is not running away scared, and you message her back, and, once again, your heart begins to stir.

You ask, "Did you read the messages that I had wrote you?"

"Yes," she replies; all that fear is gone and you make a safe mental landing, then, in a flash of thoughts, you realize that not only is she intelligent, beautiful, and artistic, but she is also understanding. She doesn't judge you for who you are; you are just a human being with a big heart in her eyes, and after that moment of realization you realize that she may be distant in another state, and that her personality shines brighter than any star.

One may feel as though they are damaged goods, which leads people to avoid laying out their cards on the table, but I just learned that there are women out there who are understanding and are not lost in the judgmental woods. For those of you that have lost hope in finding someone who will accept who you are, the trick is to stop looking, because they are in your proximity, and not so distant that your passion is squandered, because they are not far. Don't lose hope and don't let your passion refrain, because that person is out there with a beautiful brain.

Alive Awakening

The moment you locked eyes, compassion and warmth emanated from her soft gaze. Every part of you feels receptive because you know the time and space you are sharing with her is a mutual desire of both parties. The emotions that flood your brain with her in your presence makes endorphins rush like a river of happiness you haven't felt in ages. You question if this is real, when you see the crack of her smile that reveals such perfect white teeth, you accept that an angel

sits across from your mindset that can't help but factor in a level of disbelief, and as you relish every moment of her being she indeed exists within the proximity of your space.

Trivial conversation seems pointless at this point, because any dialogue would just ruin such a perfect moment in time. Your heart beats faster as you can't seem to pick a single flaw from such a magnificent woman who has chosen to accompany you on such an evening that you undoubtedly won't forget as long as your memory serves you. You can't help but take the most of this magical anomaly in existence, in a quick decision you boldly extend nervous hands across the table, and she is more than receptive as she grabs onto your hands and you feel the warmth of a soul that is undoubtedly pure.

A giant grin forms on your face, as you can't help but feel jovial and blessed. The words you want to say build inside you with tremendous pressure, and you can't hold back the dam of accumulated feelings. You finally break the silence you both have been enjoying with sentiments that stem from the core of your heart. You softly say, "Beauty, inner warmth, and compassion emanates from every part of your being, and I can't believe such a flawless entity sits before me."

This moment may just be a fragment of time, no matter what happened between us, and I will never forget the magical moment we just shared. Such angelic form makes any compliment I tell you have no gravity, because quite frankly I have never met another woman like you." Her cheeks turned red, and then in a glorious moment of passion, she reached across the table and as her soft lips pressed against

mine, I felt something I hadn't felt in years. Alive.

Budding Bloom

She has total understanding. She has no intention of branding; a heart that could leave any weak man standing. She's a beautiful woman with a mind that could lead the blind. Compassion with every word, your minds travel on similar wavelengths – she corrects your vision when it was once blurred. Your words attracted her to you; you were overly-exuberant and grandiose – you might be a mystery to her, but she has a clue. Fate, in a world of millions, brought you to meet; you cherish every moment of her speech – a soul like this is so rare it makes your heart rapidly beat.

All the social circles it took to find her, all the forums you posted in searching; you have finally found someone to whom you can emit pure emotion – a gorgeous transfer. You have to remind yourself this is just the beginning; don't jump the gun, play your cards right; this is someone for whom you are willing to be her knight. Only time will tell what will happen next; you can only hope things continue at the pace they have – you are dealing with a woman who is amazing and complex

Bestowed Beauty

She came out of nowhere, when you had recently lost a lover who is now gone. She reached out and wanted to get to know the soul behind the words she read; you thought of her as just another fan, but then you looked at her profile – and then you were stunned by that face and that flowing, dark hair. You read her original message again, and you can see intelligence behind that mind; you thank fate for putting yourself out there, and you relish your new find. She knows the way you think – your thought processes, and if she accepts you for who you are, then there just might be a spiritual link.

A million questions flood your mind: who is this soul whom was magnetized to you – she makes your cheeks turn red when your psyche is blue. She is someone you want to get to know, but you have to hold back a volcanic eruption of passion – because that's not how you will win her, that is not the fashion. You decide to give her small doses of yourself, only a paragraph per day – if you want this mortal to stay. What a delicate situation it is to meet someone who, so beautiful, inside and out, wants to know the "real you" – and all you want to do is release a joyful shout. Do you treat her like a lover, or do you turn into a cold, hard, reptilian, calculated man? You only have a few moments to devise a strategy and plan.

Women are such complicated creatures – they are filled with different desires, emotions, and hormones; it's a sad situation when you don't know what to say to her, when you both have the same thing holding you together – a skeletal structure, nothing but bones. Advice from others is, "Take it slow" – water the flower, give it sun, and let it grow.

Passion cannot be given too fast; you will turn her off mentally, and then she will be just another name of the past. After a deep breath, a moment outside in the sun – you create a subtle scheme on how this beautiful woman can be won. She has bestowed beauty; you cannot come off as egotistical, or, even worse, snooty. Just be yourself, and let time do the rest; be the book that gets read one page at a time, and then is placed right back on the shelf.

Delicate Dialogue

Attraction begins at first sight, the way she looks only makes your heart beat faster, and you approach cautiously as you utter an icebreaker that must be strategically right. You don't want to come off as arrogant or assertive, you have to choose your words wisely and not come off as furtive. Every string of sentences you murmur to her is like disarming a bomb, you want this woman to crave you, you want to gain a mutual interest, because you have been alone for so long. Finding a companion in this society is nearly impossible, everyone is looking for the perfect human being, when in reality that is a lost cause, because we are all screwed up in one way or another, one has to look for just the right amount of tolerable defects, this is a mindset that is plausible.

Even if you feel so damaged that you are "un-dateable," you are wrong, because there are so many people in this world that there is someone out there with a similar set of circumstances who will find you more than relatable. I have a high intelligence which women find attractive; they secretly yearn to produce offspring who will innately be smart like their father, so the best thing for you to do to attract women is educate yourself and be intellectually proactive. When you do come into contact with that woman whom you would like to date, open her mind with words of wisdom, and once you prove you are more than just a man with carnal desires of sex, she will most likely want to be your mate.

Don't just talk about yourself or what makes you desirable, it's not something that is impressive, it seems egotistical, narcissistic, and self-centered; rather, talk about them and show interest in what they do, because that way of doing about it is more reliable. You must not lay all your cards out on the table, women like to read men like a book, one page at a time, if you just dump all your emotional baggage to them it will instantly ruin the romance and this is no fable.

Talking to the opposite sex is akin to a soldier with a metal detector looking for landmines, you need to read her micro-expressions, you need to read her body language, you need to read between the lines of her dialogue, and most importantly, give yourself a sense of a being with a backbone, you are no invertebrate; you have a spine. When you know the time is right, when she discloses personal information about herself, that is the cue for you to lay out one of your cards on the table, you will share an intimate moment, and the both of you will not hold back emotions, this will turn the time you have spent together into a moment of wealth. This is just the beginning of the dating dance and it is just the prologue, if you play your game this way, you might just find a lover in this game of delicate dialogue.

Personal Prison

Emotional walls are built by the bricks of lovers who made conscious efforts to previously hurt you, because these bricks will only create an internal psychological defense mechanism of tactically worded sentences with specific information each time you verbalize thoughts to a potential new lover. This only builds the constant desire to keep the honeymoon period of pure warmth and a romantic entanglement that you want to be remain to perfect, because you desire this level of affection so greatly this behavior causes you do not disclose the full picture of the reality of the situation on your side of the fence.

You are choosing to guide the person you are trying to magnetize to be your lover through a mind field of emotional baggage you refuse to accept and let go, since you are afraid your past pain will be unaccepted by the person whom you are trying to romance, you will eventually have to hit a point where they step on that mine, and then they will be forced to walk away injured. They are not leaving

you because they don't accept you for your past, they now know you have guided them into a mind field, and the paranoia you instill in them about all the other dangers to them you are holding back will make you lose someone who once loved you a great deal leave your proximity forever.

You won't know why they left you, your fear will chalk it up to them not accepting you, and this will create a vicious cycle that will never end until you are in complete social solitude. The loneliness of your personal prison will force you to, later on in life, accept someone with whom you will never truly be happy, and you will have to cope with a situation that doesn't always make you happy, but it makes you happy enough just to have a warm body next to you when you lay down to sleep at night; which you willingly accept is the best you can do all because of feelings you just can't let go of past memories that bear a stigma on your soul.

The only way to break free from this cycle of unintentionally distancing yourself is by accepting that you are an organic organism who is inertly flawed, and you learn your whole life by a process of trial and error. Thus, you should not be afraid of when you guided yourself into a hurtful situation, a wrong decision, or a memory that was painful. You must accept that you are a human being, believe that you are no better than anyone else, and if someone doesn't accept you when you are upfront about a past situation then they themselves do not deserve to be with someone like you.

Lust is when someone is driven toward you out of the desirable qualities one finds in you based out of sex appeal and the desire to copulate with you due to momentary passion. Infatuation is when someone can't stop thinking about your magnetic personality and your intelligence, but that will fade when their wandering eye views something in their proximity that they would rather surround themselves with instead. Finally, love is an unconditional emotion in which you care for someone no matter what they have done in life, if you condition your emotions to fear one's love for what you have done in life; this inability of self-acceptance will filter out any true happiness you will ever have.

Compassionate Connection

Hearts that beat abnormally fast when associations that come of her and what thumps in haste suddenly becomes still, in a time when you were unable to make healthy choices, she has realigned your stubborn vision, because now you want to live forever with her and she has instilled nothing but pure power of will. Your internal empathy for every living thing made you a pacifist with no presence of hot

emotions because they are nothing but chill, if at any time in the

future anything consciously chooses hurt, because you will be ready

to shift into a dangerous mode with protective ability to render any

threat immobile with a precise skill. In a world where people cause

more injustice and actions that are wrong than a deed that is

considered ethically right, she makes you desire to create a safer

place for your true love, you will do anything in your power to

change things, because with each grouping of algorithmic words you

type you are only changing the way people think; for her, you are a

warrior putting up the strongest intellectual fight.

With each tick of the clock on your wall there builds doses of

desire you can't ignore, the tremendous sexual passion that rages

like an uncontrollable forest inside you with every measurable value

of your core, it is a hormonal-based magma that is hotter which is

fueled by the attraction of her intelligence and an undeniable beauty,

and each second makes you yearn for this woman more. That

moment where you

and her can finally be alone, the volcanic eruption of created carnal

desires will make you push her onto the bed with a loving lust, that

monster inside you will be unleashed with the tone of her moan, and as you rip her pants just down to her ankles only to prevent her from

fully spreading her legs; your alpha male-like dominance will put her

in the zone. The moment that will be greater than anything

else in your life is when your member in this pure passion has

reached the size of its apex, she has been waiting for this for such a

long time she is overflowing in feminine juices that only tell you she

is ready to accept, and the first feeling of where both of your

hormonal hopes are rewarded as every inch of you internally glides

in a satisfaction that the true emotional definition is love, but the act

can only be deemed as superlative, once-in-a-lifetime, unforgettable

sex.

Painful Pleasure

We scream at each other for an hour just so we can fuck,

arguments that are just struggles for dominance, because the anger

makes us feel alive; we like pushing our luck. Psychological games

that last for days, we are both toxic for each other, but passion is

ignited when we see the anger in each other's cold gaze. We love to

hurt and we hurt to love, at the end of the day when the war is over,

we will hold each other close, because it's no longer time to shove.

The holes in the drywall, the broken vase on the floor, the ripped-up picture of when we first met, and we both can't deny this is the aftermath of a lovers sprawl.

I am the bile that rises in your throat, you are the hole in the boat that makes it unable to float, and together we are a symphony composed with every wrong note. Do I remind you of your father, you are just as demanding as my mother, and it is because of these sick traits that we even bother. You can burn my clothes in the front yard, I will drive your new car directly into a wall, and despite this twisted love our relationship is nothing more than a maxed-out credit card. Enemies who sleep together at the end of the night, we may kiss each other before we go to sleep, but when the sun rises it will be a whole new fight.

Absent Admirations

As you inch the door shut, that devious smile slowly grows on your face, and when she sees it that's when the anticipation starts to build. You gingerly walk to her intimate proximity, as you extend your hand to gently grab the back of her neck, you play with her delicate soft hair, and gently give it a light tug. Her eyes close as she can start to feel the euphoria that is about to begin. You reach in close and kiss the crook of her neck, as you give it a soft, playful bite.

She can't help but release a moan of pleasure, you have been gone for so long, and often her dreams would be filled with the presence of your romantic company.

That bite begins to turn to light kisses, which make her tremble in the night that is about to unfold. Strong arms wrap around her body and soothe the loneliness she endured in your absence. As you both relish the essence of each other's pheromones they only cause body temperatures to rise, as the both of your breathing begins to get more intense. In a bout of alpha male passion you rip open her designer buttoned-up shirt, and the price she paid for it has no meaning in this moment of ecstasy. In a swift motion you unclasp her bra like you have done countless times before. She pulls off your shirt in a manner that is almost tactical, which now has perspiration around the underarms due to the exponentially increasing anticipation.

You both hug each other bare-chested as you lock lips, and kiss like lovers who were separated from a war that was so long ago that your memories of each other even began to fade. She tastes as you remember, and you don't want this moment to end. The distance has been brutal, when the only thing that would ruminate through your mind was getting back to the woman you loved, but now that time is here and you can relish every moment of it. You both unlock lips, you stare into her beautiful hazel eyes, and then you throw her on the bed with all your might. Panties fly off and hit the floor in record speed, and you both waste no time feeling each other in the most intimate way possible.

Moans of pleasure are muffled in the depths of the goose-down pillow, and you become something rather primal as you dominate the woman you love with every ounce of energy in your body. She uncontrollably screams into the pillow, and then you have your release. She turns around and looks at you, her cheeks are red as her breathing is heavy, and the satisfaction on your face couldn't be seen anywhere else on this earth. You crawl up next to her, wrap your body around hers, and you both lay there in complete bliss.

You try to store this memory deep in your consciousness, so it is never lost by the time that makes you forget, it is something you went so long without, that if you were ever separated again, all you want is a recollection to bring you back to this magical moment. You both drift away in complete happiness as you slowly fall asleep, because the thing you wanted most of all was to be next to her one last time.

Magnificent Magnetism

It is an unseen force, it pulls one person to another, it makes two pieces whole, it is what makes everything attract, it is what leads everything to its destination, it guides things to their course. Whether it is the articulate thoughts of one human to another, whether it is the actions of someone in motion, whether it is kindness you see in someone's heart; it is what makes one person become someone else's brother. It is a law of creation, it is what brings things together, and it pulls distant objects to a whole and creates a unified station. It can be your style, your way of thinking; whatever the draw it collects all things living or not to a pile.

It makes someone contact you out of the blue, it is the desire for one person to get to know another, and it is the societal glue. Extroverts are natural magnets because they say what is on their mind, how can your thoughts be heard if you don't express yourself, how will you attract someone who views you as a golden find. Introverts have a tougher time magnetizing people to them, they are mute in their thinking, and they will never find their match, because people will have to dig past their emotional wall to see if they are an undiscovered gem. Never silence yourself, never hold back who you are, be open to the world, don't fear what people think of you, otherwise you will be that dusty book that remains unread just left on the shelf.

Be loud like the beat of a drum, don't fear rejection no matter who you are, because this world is big enough that someone will like your tune and join along with you as you hum. The people who reject who you are as a person are not the people you want to be with anyway, you want someone with your similarities; you want a common bond that will make them be by your side and they will forever stay. Open yourself up, be the peacock that blossoms its plumage, let yourself shine for who you really are, and you will be filled to the top in your lonely cup. Don't let the fear of someone walking away from who you are, look in the sky at night, there are so many beams of light; you will be bound to find your star.

Let nature work in your favor, beam the core of who you are to the masses no matter how damaged you may feel, because there is someone out there who will like the taste of your flavor. There are currently seven billion people on this planet, there is someone out there for you no matter how grim things may feel, it is a numbers game, and you need to attract them to you, all while being ready for rejection, and tough as granite. Use the laws of nature to your advantage and harness the magnetism, you will lose those who don't deserve you, and those who do will make you shine bright like light through a prism.

Keepsake Kiss

It starts out with sexual attraction: what a face, what a body – it causes an internal reaction. You want to get to know the essence behind those powerful eyes – and you feed her pure truth, and not a single lie. Hair that flows in such a delicate fashion; she is naturally beautiful – she is not dolled-up, which only ignites more inward passion. You sit across from each other; it is your first time seeing her, face-to-face – something inside tells you she would be a perfect mother.

You begin to converse; you discuss the small things in life, nothing perverse. The conversation shifts on a deeper level; the way she thinks only makes you revel. You start to develop an intellectual bond, with a woman so attractive she makes you more than fond. You get nervous, because you may have found the one – and you are more than in it for mere fun.

You begin to stutter, your palms begin to sweat; you are in disbelief that this person exists, whom you just recently met. Like two puzzle pieces that fit perfectly, you both build a picture that looks like something tangible – and you don't see this ever becoming frangible. Dinner is over, and you pay for the check – you want to show her that you can support her, monetarily...and that you are not a financial wreck.

Your heart beats faster as you both rise from the table; you know what you want to do, but are you fully capable? You begin to exit the restaurant, and walk her to her car; you know the moment is coming when you will both split off in different directions – you want her so close, but she is only going to go far. You say something sentimental, about the times you just shared, and you can see it in her eyes; she appreciates it, and you are not just putting her on with womanizing lies.

What comes from the heart will penetrate the soul; when you say something that is just another line from your book, you will never reach your goal. There is a moment of silence; it makes every part of you nervous, because this could be the end – dating is such a complicated science. Then she sees the desire in your eyes; you look back at her like she is the prize. Then, in a moment, you tell yourself: it is now or never. You disregard every voice in your head – and lean in close, as her cheeks turn red. Then, the moment you have waited for an eternity to happen – and in this case, you did not miss; you come in close, smell her essence, and you both share a passionate, loving kiss.

Kind Kindness

She loved a man who I never understood, she showed me kindness in a cruel world, I fell in love within the first few times we talked, but could I be the man to guide her into womanhood? She was a golden-haired deviant with eyes of hazel and teeth as white as they come, she understands you when most might turn the other way, and you are bold enough to uproot yourself and venture to the land where she is from. You are prepared to weather any storm that may come your way, she has captured your heart, and there is nothing on this Earth that will make you sway.

She is bold, passionate, and filled with mirth; you will do anything to please her, when things get thin you will show her girth. You have lived so many lives you have lost count of who you really are, you are lost in this world and she is your compass, and you feel that together you can both venture far. Your mind is warped like a record that simply will not play, she understands you like no other woman could, and in your world of sadness she makes you gay. She harbors something in her heart that makes you want to come close, she is a kind woman, and at times when she makes you speechless your vocabulary becomes verbose.

She likes all the things a little boy ever could, she plays ball, gets in the mud, and, for her, you are prepared to do things you felt you never would. If she loves this man so much, if her mind is built like a technological mousetrap, you cant wait until the day when you can feel her touch. She may not feel the way you do about her, you will give her all your love, and pray to the heavens that something inside her starts to stir. Kind kindness is what drew you in, you are prepared to go to war for her, and you will last through thick or thin.

Tempting Touch

For so long I have wanted to feel your healing touch. Without your love, I need a crutch. You are beautiful in every way – from the things you do, from the things you say. It's not sex I'm looking for; I'm looking for your love that will soothe me to the core. I'm living in a lonely space and time, and you are perfect, you are in your prime. I want to kiss your silky skin, and that's only where I will begin. Save me from this nightmare that I'm living in; rescue me, darling – you don't know where I have been. My life can be a scary place, and the only thing that can save me is your beautiful face.

Rescue me, baby, from this insanity that I go through; your presence keeps me together like the strongest glue. All I pray for is that you will come join me by my side, because it's been such a long, scary ride. Every day without you is a constant fight; you are the only one who can make me right. The life I have lived has been such a horrible journey; if I spend another day without you, I fear they will take me away on a gurney. I need you to save me from the people who surround me; please don't ignore my plea.

When I see you, there are diamonds in your eyes; I know I'm bronze, but you, baby, are first prize. Don't leave my side, you are the only one who turns the madman sane; your words truly pacify my brain. I want to give you the world and everything you deserve; you help me avoid the accident as you help me swerve. For so long I have wanted to feel your healing touch; you aren't interested in money, which is why I love you so much. You're beautiful inside and out; you have a tremendous capacity to love, without a doubt.

I want to feel the soft peck of your lips, as I gently caress your hips. I want to make you feel like a queen, because you are the one who powers this machine. I will protect you, never defect you, and make you happy when you are blue. You are the world to me, you are my sanity, and the things I want to do to you may seem like a profanity. Open me, make me love again, and help me let the emotion in – all while I caress your silky skin. I need you to soothe me, I need you to woo me; I need your love and nothing more, because this life has been such a horrendous road I have traveled – and with you by my side I won't become unraveled.

Reviving Responses

Hold me close. Don't let me go. The show is over, and it's the true me I want you to know. I know you will fear what you don't understand, so as I tell you this I want you to hold my hand. I have just been reflecting a personality that I think you will psychologically accept. This whole relationship has been an entire act; I am a master manipulator, and now you know the fact. I always loved you, it was more than just sex; but it's time for me to come true. I change on a daily basis – call it an evolutionary trait. I can't control what I am; at my core I am nothing but a blank slate.

I've surfed so many social circles, but then when I found you, I wanted you to love me, I wanted to be true. In my eyes you are beautiful in every way, so I did nearly everything to make you stay. You made someone with no emotions finally feel love; with you by my side I could fight any battle, I could rise above. You were everything to me, and I would do anything for you; I was there for you when you would cry yourself to sleep, I opened your eyes so you weren't a sheep. I helped you evolve your soul, and to control you was never my goal. I'll never forget our first kiss; you made a dead man feel alive, and that moment in time I will forever miss.

Now you have gone away to live another life, and you left me as an individual with nothing but inner strife. I will never find someone to replace how special you were; with you now absent, all my days have bled together. Your presence was a gift from God, and now all I see in the mirror is an individual who was so difficult to be with, I can only feel one feeling – and that is that I am nothing but flawed.

Fortunate Fate

We met by a random chance. Your mind was open enough for us to verbally dance. You accepted me for who I truly am; my feelings for you are immense and they are no sham. I want to rescue you, and be your protector; I have the power and I will be your deflector. You are a flower that blossomed in such harsh conditions, I will bring you to a better place, and that is my ambition. The pain you have gone through is a thing of the past; we have created a bond that will eternally last. Your nightmare is over, you can wake up now; you can escape from your environment, and I will show you how. You will be my queen, you will be endlessly adored; together we cut the normal bullshit, and we have reached the most beautiful scene. You are a treasure fate provided me with – this isn't a dream, nor is it a myth. We will flourish together as we build a wonderful life; you will no longer have to deal with the daily strife. I can't wait to feel your touch; you may be distant now, but I will come to you and kick in the clutch.

Pure Perfection

As I gaze into your bright accepting eyes, I can't believe something so perfect is of an organic origin, because when I see your glowing essence only the truth comes out of my mouth rather than the usual string of lies. You are a golden ratio of natural perfection, my heart pounds in my chest as my skin tingles in your presence, and without a question you have every ounce of my affection. Your brain fires at the soothing rate of a metronome, you make all the pain this existence created evaporate from my memory, and the only thing I can think about is how I want to make you my princess and take you home.

The vibrations that are dispatched with an understanding consciousness emanates to those around you, a rare mineral that would take millions of years to excavate, because you are the star of the show on the red carpet; every moment in this life time is your debut. You may be a woman but your true classification is an anomaly to those who are lucky enough to discover, anyone's head turns upon catching a glimpse, when they see you they can't help but try to stay in your proximity, because within your stunning, magnetic sphere they wish to hover.

With a soft pleasant voice that pleases any ear and a demeanor that screams class, you may be a person stronger than any manufactured metal, but there is no one on this earth who won't treat you as delicate as glass. You make the sane man mad, the rich man poor, and the man in a pit of sorrow feel nothing but glad. It's not
your sex appeal that makes you such a prize, you are the whole package, and you don't belong on surface of this planet; rather, high above where everyone can admire you in the skies. Perfection has been redefined, even when you go back to Heaven where you belong, because of the short moment in time you shared with me; you will never leave my mind.

Learning Love

Some of us love to hate, hate to love, and we fight feeling any emotion that can help us feel anything in-between. Rage is addiction that can blind us, deafen us, and label us; when, deep down inside, we are just looking for the comfort that others can offer. The trick to escaping this lifestyle is accepting how we all have the capacity to love, and that those who surround us are just waiting for you to let the warmth in. In this cold, harsh world, those who can learn to love will find it to be their salvation; those who continue to hate will be destroyed by that emotion, because it poisons the heart, the mind, and the soul. The more love you let in, the more it will destroy your ability to hate – and the happier you and the people around you will be. We all suffer; so why drag it out by having toxic emotions that will only sabotage you in the end?

Love's Labor

At first sight, you are infatuated; you haven't had a lover in so long, her soul permeates your core and leaves you saturated. You can't hold back; you explode like a volcano of love, spreading passion all over her tender surface. That lava, as hot as it is, creates a fire in every part of her that it touches; that fire spreads to other areas, she grabs onto your essence and clutches. Every moment you share with her is special in every way; she gives you butterflies, and you hope with all your heart that this one will stay.

As you get to know each other, you slowly and slowly reveal more cards of your hand – hoping that she will accept every part of you, so she comes to join your intellectual land. This has nothing to do with having sex; your hormones play no part in this process, because it is a soul mate you are looking to possess. With each communication that passes, you are not aware; but this love you are feeling is only building to an apex – a crescendo that is invisible to you, and these feelings will only rip and tear.

Then it happens: during all this delicate communication, this fragile process of words strung together triggers emotions and associations. You reveal one card too many. Just like a match onto a pile of wood and gasoline – everything you have built, everything you shared, goes up in flames; she rejects you, and you are burned, nothing will heal that scorched heart – there is not enough Vaseline. You are filled with rage, horror, and you wish a million times you wouldn't have said the thing you did to drive her in the opposite direction; all you wanted in this world was her unlimited affection.

Just like the list of all the others that you had admired, she is now another name on the page whom you want to forget – and you just lost your job as her suitor, you were fired. The pain you feel won't last long, because this world is so big it will only be a matter of time whereupon your brilliance attracts another candidate to your place in space; you have to remind yourself that you did everything right and nothing wrong. Love comes and goes, and, soon enough, you will meet another woman who will once again lift you off your toes.

Loveless Lover

I have always admired you from afar. The way your hair blows in the wind, the way your eyes glow like a star. It kills me to see you to destroy yourself, as you take another bottle of pills off the shelf. You will try anything to soothe your pain, and everyday you lose your footing, as there is nothing you gain. You have blocked out all emotion for so long; you feel dead inside, you feel weaker than you do strong. Life has been a brutal journey for you, but if you let the love in you will have your breakthrough. You don't have to run anymore; the nightmare is over, you can once again feel the warmth in your core. Just collapse on the floor, take a deep breath, cry it out, and close your door. You can beat the agony that you feel by letting the love in, and no longer will tears run down your chin. The world you have been blocking out for so long has been waiting for you to hear the words of the therapeutic song. Once you realize that none of this was your fault, you will begin to push forward – and you will finally be able to open the hope that lies in your inner vault.

You will realize life is such a beautiful thing that you don't know why you go back and forth on the depressive swing. Once you open your mind, you can unlock your heart, and that's when the flood of feelings will start. You won't need to numb yourself anymore because you will no longer be in pain; now go outside and wash away "the old you" in the pouring rain. This is the time of your rebirth; now that the worst is over, you can finally stand tall as you walk the Earth.

I prayed for you to outgrow your torment; you have, and there's no need to look back and lament. Be the person you wished you could be; you've established your roots, so grow tall like a tree.

Satisfying Scents

Women are amazing on every level, they cook for us when we are hungry, they take the time out of their day to take us to the hospital when we have to have those polyps removed from our colon, and they love us when we are feeling low; it only makes us revel. They clean our clothing and wash our underwear, they take the kids to school, they record football on DVR, and you know that the woman whom you married is something more than rare. They keep our heads straight when we start to go crazy, they make sure we are never late for work, they pack lunches for us, and they force us to get off our ass when we get lazy. They are our angels from the first day we met, they pay the bills on time, they get the brown stains out of your underwear, and they always sooth us with wise words so we don't fret.

You make her breakfast in bed, you rub her feet, you buy her stuff from Bed Bath & Beyond, and she even let you built that backyard shed. She doesn't mind when you pass gas, she fixes you extra gravy because she knows you love it, all your socks are always clean, and you even don't mind when she throws your way a bunch of sass. She will clean up the dog poop when it is clearly your turn, she's not a boozehound, she always stays a lady, and she never yells at you when you let the salmon burn. You forgot last Mother's Day, you made it up to her by buying her a card at a gas station and she didn't seem to care, she will always shave your hairy neck, and when it comes to buying the gas she knows you missed your last promotion, so she doesn't force you to pay.

You kiss her with passion every time, you buy her that dishwasher detergent she likes, and she loves it with you talk nonsense to her, especially when you manage to rhyme. You were late on the rent last week, you still need to fix that dishwasher valve, you missed your dental appointment last week and insurance is not going to cover it, and you still have to fix that kitchen sink leak. There is one thing that makes your relationship last every year, you may me be a clumsy idiotic husband, but there is one thing that you intimately share that to your eye will always bring a tear.

She sits on your face every time you get up for your job, it's for a good thirty minutes, sometimes you can't quite breathe, but that pussy intoxication makes the rod in your pants oscillate in circles and you begin to tremendously throb. There is something about those pheromones that she is releasing from below, you want your face to live in her reproductive gash, you may have a safety word, but you can't breathe enough to mutter it, so you just enjoy the ride just before you blow.

A relationship can be a wonderful thing, when two mutual people join together and live in a common place, and every day they get the pleasure of seeing their loving face. Spiritual harmony can be a blessing from a higher power, you will never take your relationship for granted, and every day you will come home from work to give her the most desirable flower.

Simple Sapiosexuals

Unlike a majority of the population, there are a certain few of us who don't let our hormones dictate our copulation. The cattle of humanity go out to clubs, go out to bars, go out to strip clubs, and are only attracted to vanity. Some of you out there only desire sex when you need to stimulate our minds – you need to make us think, you need to make us ponder, you need to make us wonder, and you need intelligence to get the treasure inside the intimacy of our kind.

Read a book, watch a foreign film, listen to classical music, and don't tell us which rapper has the best hook. Intelligence is sexy – and when you present yourself as a dumbass with no class, there is no chance of getting in our pants. You are uneducated, you are dull, you are boring, you are ninety percent of the population; we won't let you near us, and you won't be touching us. The best sex comes from someone with a brain; you say something beautiful and bright, and we will fuck you all night.

Other than that, you are just cattle following the masses. You associate with lower forms of living beings, and that only sends the rest of us fleeing. Unless you educate yourselves, grow your brains, raise your bars – we will be untouchable: not close, but far. We each have the capacity to raise our consciousness; it's only a select few who choose to actually do so. If you cannot learn, then you will be stuck with a woman who only wants your seed; she wants you to fill her up, and spread your stupid breed.

If you want someone who will change your life, the answer is simple: become something saucy, witty, raffish, clever, dapper, stylish, dashing – and you will meet someone who will make your heart and brain aroused; then you will make the most passionate love, and you will both be roused.

Sexually Stimulated

We look eye-to-eye, soul-to-soul, and spirit-to-spirit; passions build and you both begin to softly touch, there is no need to talk, you both want it as such. At the first moment of contact, the anticipation builds; just feeling your lover leaves you with stimulated chill. You lean in close, and both your lips link, from that moment all you can do is ponder everything you want to do to her, make her feel like a desired treasure, you will only give her what she does prefer. Your kissing becomes more passionate, like a rapid firing machine gun, with each and every striking you show her that this isn't just going to be some lay, rather something deeply compassionate.

In the heat of oral contact, clothes start to fall to the floor, and your lover's mania drives you both to want more and more. Tongues become intertwined, you are both in the moment, and relish every moment of this time. She can't help but touch the thing that makes you a man, and you are at full tilt for her, she fondles it in her hand. You begin to touch her breasts; you are gentle with this flower, as you just gently caress. You begin to suck on her bosoms; she is so stimulated her nipples are hard; your mouth works every inch of them, and then you pull off her panties and discard. You touch the part of her that makes her able to be a mother, she is filled with feminine dew, you caress her soft folds, and you can but get on your knees to take in her scent, pheromones, and taste her intoxicating personal feminine stew.

When you are making love, every moment happens so fast; you are both in the moment of pure bliss, and in a blink of an eye two hours of pleasure seemed like only a minute has passed. For him, it's external pleasure, as he gets pleasure from the outside; for her, it is internal, and she's enjoying it from the inside. What makes this heated moment so beautiful? They are also enjoying each other on a mental level, because it's the way angels make love with no presence of the devil. Sure, there may be some dark presence under the sheets, but for them it is only a treat. They are both sexually stimulated, every moment is heavenly, and they are both elated.

Never Noble

She said she would always love you no matter the condition, you could truly be yourself around her and you never had to act, because dating her was never an audition. You knew there was something going on by the way you behaved, you started to go into psychological testing quite frequently, because you wanted to know what was wrong so you could be saved. All your life it was hard for you to find the right girlfriend, when you found her you seemed the like perfect match, and you wanted to be together until the day both of your lives would end. She could always tell you were just a little boy inside, she was also a little girl whom you would have to guide, and since you were both children at heart; you wanted for her to be the one who would be your bride.

After each year that would pass you would get a different diagnosis, they would shove pills down your throat from nearly every pharmaceutical company, and you started to exhibit the signs of somewhat frequent psychosis. You started to become chaotic, stubborn, and in general hard to please, she would carry out my high demands as she did the best to appease, but then over time my heart became a locked and she did not have the keys. Her love for me put her on a constant rollercoaster of emotion, sometimes I would be the most loving guy in the world and she loved me with devotion, and other times I was a selfish asshole and would do nothing but create a commotion.

After realizing that this cycle simply would not end, you could not bare the woman you loved to undergo this torment that you did not intend, and this was unacceptable behavior that you could not defend; you would rip her up she could only just mend. After the breakup, she had to leave you for another distant land, you could not even speak to her after the both of you disband, and because of that silence you would be vilified; from her heart you would always be banned. When you would muster up the strength to call her, there would be a new diagnosis on your tongue every time, and this would solidify in her mind that you were a hopeless saboteur; she would forget all the goodtime because now they would only be a blur. Then came the day where you actually figured out what was wrong, you finally came out of the woodwork to reveal you understand the mystery that had been lifelong, and after hearing your label she did not care if you were now strong; she blocked you from her social media no matter how far you have come along.

She had changed from the loving, caring, and understanding woman that she had been, she took all the memories that used to be and discarded them in the trash bin, because she has started over and she with you she does not want to begin. Despite the fact you were the only one who would help with her grief from being rape you are considered broken and not even worth being taped, and she

acts like there were never happy times that you had and that she was

lucky she escaped. In the end she showed who she really was;

nothing noble. She may have provided you with warmth, but she

was harmful and radioactive to your heart; like Chernobyl.

"How long were we friends? I only have been counting the number of days since we became enemies."

"It's not a drug problem, but rather, an 'I am an organism in a machine' problem."

"The slaves of ego who await the notifications from their overlord; no more than bits of data collected by the sum of intelligence for the existing horde."

TWO

WHEN ONE'S PRIORITIES ARE WAKING UP TO KILL MORE CREATURES THAN THEY SAVE, ABSORBING MORE INTELIGENCE THROUGH PLEASURE THAN PHYSICAL DRIVE ON EVERY THOUGHT WAVE, AND LYING TO THOSE WHO ONLY NEED TO HEAR THE TRUTH THEY CRAVE; THIS ONLY SPEAKS IN VOLUMES ABOUT THE FUTRE THAT THESE REPEATED ACTIONS WILL PAVE...

"Conforming is adapting in fear of what you really are, because you don't believe you are powerful enough to live on your own without the insight of the pack."

"You raise your monsters and then they will raze you."

SOCIETY

Dividing Divisions

We have two ways to look at the world: through addition or division. We often choose to divide things, which I think stems from our "gatherer" instinct from which we have not quite yet evolved. For so long we had to divide the world up filtering things that were good for us from the things that would cause us harm. We had to pay particular attention to what exactly we were putting in or near our bodies.

Certain foods were edible, but certain foods were not. Certain plants had healing effects on the body, and certain plants would cause us to die. Since the birth of our universal consciousness, we no longer need to divide everything up into little categories, as we all just log on and become one. Sure, we have divisions in thought, but only because we have all lived disparate lives so we all view things a little differently.

The true evolutionary trait that we need to accept is the ability to add up the world around us, rather than dissecting it piece-by-piece. Once we do the addition, we will realize that all of our divisionary numbers actually just add up to one big number. We are one organism that lives in many different bodies. Anything that can feel the emotion of pain is alive in nature. Rather than dividing up all of our pain, we need to start adding it together and finally come to the realization that we are all in some kind of toil.

That's the meaning of life: to experience the pain of living. The only way we can cope with that pain is by adding all of our love together and living as one giant creature, rather than as billions of small ones. Placing labels on things only divides us and keeps us from evolving into what we can truly be. It is up to each individual to choose the intellectual consensus we need to add on a daily basis, or to continue down our instinctual path to separate everything into groups.

The truth boils down to a pure fact that every nationality has the power to change the world, and that a genius does not have a color or creed. The more we divide each other, the longer we will hold each other back – which inevitably means that we are killing ourselves, slowly, through one singular mathematic notion. Change the way you do your math as a human being, and you will change your surroundings for the better. Would you rather have one delicious apple, or half of an apple that is rotten because it was divided long ago?

Societal Symbiosis

We live our lives in separation; we let small differences divide us, we try to take on the world in a one-man army mindset, and because of this notion our lives are filled with only small doses of validation. If you can be wise enough to realize you have blind spots in your daily routine, if you can accept that you are a flawed individual repeating the same mistakes, you can fix your situation if you merge with another who makes you keen. Just like the Yin and the Yang the two complete opposites are combined as one, there is not one way of life, there is every way of life, and if you join together with someone in a symbiotic relationship there is no battle in life that can't be won.

Joining two forces together as one functioning organization, you can do the things that others can't, and together you have a mutually beneficial relationship; together, you form a humanistic nation. I once lived a life of pure solitude, I tried to do everything by myself, and I tried to fight in this system of the survival of the fittest; I was overwhelmed by life's multitude. I kept all my ideas inside my head, I shared no information with anyone, and soon I found myself in a situation where I was hoping my suicidal actions would leave me dead. I had no partner in life, no one to build anything with, no one to accomplish goals with as a team, and no one to enjoy the small rewards I would get with; I was alone in strife.

Then one day, someone saw the brilliance I had to provide, they saw me suffering alone, and they became my friend and together we walked in the same stride. I helped him with his troubles, he helped me with mine, and then we became symbiotic; not two people but one functioning unit as we both became human doubles. When I was at a low point he would get me high, and when life weighed him down I would enable him to fly. Together we became something more than friends, we collaborated on everything even though we are total opposites, and then we achieved success together and there was nothing stopping us; there would be no end. Animals do this all the time, in the ocean there are fish that live off of bigger fish, sustaining themselves from dirt that accumulates, one fish is fed, and the other fish is cleaned of grime.

There is no reason humans can't adopt this method of survival, there is no need to fight one another, we can help each other out, and not be another one's rival. Sustaining together in a mutually beneficial way, one always helps the other one, the favor is returned in time, and together both people live happily, and together they stay. I would not be the man I am today writing these words you read now, you need to find your tolerable opposite, and living in symbiosis is the process you need to accept, by living in mutual harmony and when someone offers to help, just do one thing: allow.

Masculine Man

With flesh that has been forged into muscle for looks that appeal, to attract the opposite sex with a physique that marketing and airbrushing makes a body seem ideal, and for the men who tirelessly mold their form into something that is unreal. With wallets emptied at trendy stores that make you appear to have class, from the protein powder consumed before every workout to make you appear to have more mass, and all this is done in hopes of finding nothing more than a superficial lass. The expensive automobiles purchased to prove to others you have worthwhile career, the elite credit cards with no spending limit when they are handed to the cashier, and it's all just a facade to impress their fellow peer.

With a mentality brewing notions that everything they do should be treated with respect, with bloated egos that cloud the mind from thinking about those they neglect, every argument must be won because they never can take disrespect, and all this behavior makes them lose the ability to live in a society where they connect. Every choice must be correct even if it is made from a half-brewed notion, when the reality of the matter is that it will only cause other people to cause a commotion, and they still will endlessly stand by what they think is right with a fervid devotion. They will lust for the blood of their enemies on the battlefield, even when the politics that guide their destruction will later be revealed, and the ones who needlessly died due to carnal desire will never be healed.

The emotions that brew inside concrete heads like a chemical stew, when some are so gentle they make warriors into children whom they subdue, others are so volatile the rage inside them makes them break through, and then there are the feelings that pacify a madman to only subdue. Some men lust over women and power, others feel only love when they pick a fresh flower, some may envy another man's fortune and pride which only makes them scour, and when green takes hold of a being they only turn sour. Anger only brings on a feeling of eternal emptiness of one's soul, they hate what the media tells them to be which consumes Humanity as a whole, and when fear of an uncertain future is on the path ahead they are afraid to take the stroll. Surprise is when they get what they don't deserve but somehow obtain, sadness consumes us when there is no one to love them which causes emotional strain, and disgust is what should not happen but does anyway; they are only left to complain.

Sex is what causes everything in society to work like a clock, they dress nice, they groom themselves to be dapper, they pay for expensive restaurants, and they even give false compliments when they talk.

They pretend they are things they are not, they pretend this is how it will always be which is just a plot, and they are just trying to achieve a single sexual moment with things that exist in this world that can be bought. They tell them lies, they will comfort their cries, when they are dumb they pretend to be wise, and if the woman does not fall for it the man will do nothing but despise. It's the societal game of copulation that we play, it is the delicate dance we do to make them want to stay, it is all for a moment of bliss for this extravagant display, and then when the sheets are sweaty he will take off his mask and she feels it was a mistake; the sexual art of emotional betray.

Wonderful Women

In soft inviting eyes that give you an entrance to voids of energy that can tell no lies, they bring you deep into her soul so expansive that it is limitless in size, and the only thing you can see is a being who has lived for so long that she can't be anything but wise. With a smile that beams of teeth that glow, with a soft laugh that tells you she is ready for the show, and with every passing moment she is in your presence without a doubt she is the one you want to eternally know. She makes your emotions override your brain, she is the one you will endlessly toil as you pull what makes the world go round which is the never ending chain, and with every action in your power until the day you die she will be the one you try to obtain.

Her touch heals your aching wounds that simply will not heal, her worldly desires are what drive you to steal, for her you will suffer and put up with any ordeal, and you will pretend the whole time like it is no bother because of the pain you will conceal. After a twelve-hour labor that nearly breaks your spirit everyday, when you come home and feel her tender kiss upon your weather-beaten lips it is what always makes you stay, and it is because of this passion you feel that makes your heart beat fast; she's the woman who you love and it's hard for you to be away. When you lean in close and smell her pheromones that make you weak in the knees, you cannot help but relish this moment as your entire body begins to freeze, this is the reason why you will do anything for this woman who you wish you appease, and even though every man's heart is a lock his woman's scent is are his keys.

Her face is like a sculpture that was crafted with perfection by the finest artist from every angle, beautiful features like this cause wars among men that drive one another to go to battle and relentlessly mangle, perfection in such an individual causes jealously among egos that cause two sides to draw weapons and decide to tangle, and in the end the standing man who remains victorious gets to grab this jewel of his eye and they both retire to romantically entangle. It takes the perfect combination of genetics to create a woman who is desired by every onlooking eye, these women who are so flawless in every way will capture a man's heart with such disregard for their own longevity and for these specimens they will be willing to die, fathers of these flawless creations will send hoping suitors a heart-wrenching deny, and the one who will win such a princess is the one who will fight to the death for her and never comply.

They have bodies that personify perfection in every way from delicate feet, silky skin, and hips that would make any man's judgment become flawed, with genitals perfectly designed for reproduction; the truest man with whom they lead on via flawless facade, and with breasts so perfect in form they had to be created by an act of God. These are they types of beauties who could make a civilization crumble, these are the types of goddesses who make even a knight with blood on his sword nervously stumble, these are the creatures of creation who make even the man with the biggest ego nothing but humble, and these are the wonderful women who cause even all-around balanced men to trip on their own feet as in their presence they nervously tumble.

Situational Stigmas

In a kingdom of fear where everyone else is afraid of the unknown you had open eyes and open ears and an inviting tone. You allowed me to interact with the core of your essence, you allowed me to spread my wings and show you what I am fully capable of, and this act was akin to freeing the dove. I showed you what an extremely complicated mind was capable of – how, inside this curse of my existence brews something capable of only the most passionate forms of love.

You may be a distance from me, but that is just the way things should be, what happens from this moment on should only happen organically. You are such an amazing find in my eyes, of all the social circles I have surfed to get to you, you seem like the biggest catch; the ultimate prize. You have an amazing understanding for who I am and what I might be fully capable of, but this is only the beginning you have tried many fits in the past, but perhaps this is finally the glove. You need to be cherished on all accounts; a woman with your capacity should be cherished in every amount. I am often forced to detach myself from a female-oriented situation, because they are just fans of my writing, I am just their current fixation.

The way we met, it just seemed too pure, you were apprehensive at first, but then I showed you my ability to cure. I am a healer, and you must know I am not like any man, I have a plan of attack, and now that I have found you: this is my last stand. Tell me what you desire, and I will try and give it to you within the compounds of my empire. I am excited that I have found a new woman to rekindle my inner fire, with your help I will write amazing things – you will be my beam of guiding light, as our intelligence reflects off each other – I am a word warrior and I have just begin to fight. I look forward to seeing where this mutual understanding goes, and I promise every moment, I will fill up your mental cup and keep you on your toes.

Just last night I ended a relationship with a woman from across the seas. She tried her hardest, but she just could not wrangle me. I am a free spirit, I go and do what I please, she tried to bind me emotionally, and because of that I only left her on her knees. If this ever becomes too much, just let me know, and I will try for a more delicate touch. You are currently the one whom I wish to communicate with, our age is on the money, and I think that this is no myth. Let's see where these times take us, and let's see how strong a magnetic force can make us continually discuss.

I am excited for the times ahead on this road, there is a bright future, and so many have tried to understand me but I carry a tremendous load. You are dealing with a weight of the ages, and I will help you understand every action I make, as you read with me and turn the pages. Let's look forward to intellectual companionship and this is one boat that I will not let tip. Follow my words and me; together we shall aesthetically guide the herds.

Silent Sadness

Our society promotes one emotion every day, we overindulge on foods that make us hate our appearance, we buy things clever marketing makes us believe we need, what we see in the mirror is anything but beautiful, the way we dress ourselves has to be approved by our peers, and we try to soothe any pain we feel with drugs, and the last thing we worry about is self-perseverance. We let such trivial items dictate our self-esteem, the way we view ourselves in the mirror only affects our current mood, and most of the time we are not even satisfied in the previous night's dream.

Such pointless things try to distract us from what truly gives us joy, the latest electronics, the kind of car we drive, the house we live in, and the newest thing to play with which is just an oversized mechanical toy. These diversions try to alter what makes us unhappy with our existence, whether it's a failing marriage, a dead end job, a dying relative with a bad health condition, or a negative outlook on life that makes you pessimistic with endless persistence.

The reality of our human nature in these current times we live in, a large percentage of us are unhappy with our situations, so many of us take antidepressants, and we feel that the things we do to try to lessen the pain of our sadness is inherently a sin. The remedy for this internal grief is fairly simplistic, as kind people we need to share with others the effect their kindness and wealth of spirit has on us, emotions are contagious and other people make us happy, and thus we give love to those who can bring us up, and use the warmth in their spirit to make your attitude of this situation more optimistic.

Expressing to someone how special he or she makes you feel, it is the beginning of becoming a special person yourself, and statistically the one to whom you open up has most likely at some point in their life gone through a similar ordeal. Silent sadness is in itself a good lie, pretending not to be sad, if you do a good job can be a positive thing, you will fake it until you make it, and all you have to do is smile; happy thoughts is all you need to try.

Most of us hide behind that face, it's a camouflage for our grief by wearing that cheerful mask, it becomes almost second nature for you to put on the façade, we have gotten so good at pretending everything is fine, but the reality of the situation is a scattered brain from endless sorrow, and we are mentally all over the place. The easiest way for us to wear this mask is through the act of silence, what we often forget is everyone is sad to some extent, if you expressed what was actually on your mind you might just find a person in the same boat, when you bottle up so much eternal misery, one can get verbally abusive, or possibly show inanimate objects small outbursts of violence.

If you just came to the realization that you are not alone with your emotional pain, you would express yourself more frequently to others, you would find others who are just as miserable as you, then you would feel the strength in numbers, you will find comfort in someone who has already walked down that road, and then a human connection will be made with a friendship to gain. Be brave about your pain, take a page from an extrovert, break the silence and vocalize your grief, you will find that others will come out of the woodwork, and with the unity of your fellow man will help you end your silent sadness; you will sustain.

Determining Deviation

Our society is all about reward bands. If you jump through this hoop, you get a reward. If you do this job, you get a reward. If you say something that makes people laugh or smile, you get a reward. If people post the right things on your social network, you get a reward. We need to evolve past the notion that has been engrained in us since we were children – how if you do the right thing, you will get a reward. What if your reward was deviating from what you would normally get rewarded for, and, in turn, the deviation was a reward itself? Lacking something that is constantly driving you to get the next reward is true freedom, and then that freedom is your next reward.

Critical Climate

On a global scale today's social climate is in a critical state, the way we act within today's society will have a tremendous impact on future generations, everyday our actions ripple through space and time, and every thing we do, unknowing to us, carries significant weight. When we teach our offspring that "life is not fair," it reinforces that way of thinking that only conditions them to accept defeat, they learn to give up when they have to go against the grain, it creates stagnated thinking patterns, it molds them into accepting a self-built rut, and it trains them to stay on the ground when they are knocked down, rather than building a stronger will inside themselves, which would train them to get right back up on their feet.

If we accept that those currently in power will always remain in power, it furthers the notion that there is nothing we can do as a whole to dislodge them from power when they are obviously abusing it, when in reality they should be ready to fight for what is right, rather than instinctually preparing to cower. We create a self-fulfilling reality, where the masses will settle for the menial, it makes people accept existences of tedious labor and a lack of passion, which is what slaves accept as their mode and mentality.

Monotony that is accepted by everyone who swallows its pill, a life of servitude and unhappiness, people who would rather ride the escalator of life, rather than to take the effort involved to just climb the hill. We are on the cusp of hierarchies becoming obsolete, interpersonal links made through emerging social communities will be the way, and that is how the people of the future will begin to meet. When people with similar problems start to share their own travails and trials, we join together as a unified sum and offer each other potential solutions, once you help someone who knows exactly what that lifestyle is like, and it is those kind of relationships formed which will make you both travel down a new road of life for an unlimited length of miles.

Those types of human bonds create a brotherhood that lasts forever, you will commit to staying in touch throughout the duration of your tribulations, the primal superiority inherent in traditional hierarchies becomes irrelevant, and together you can overcome any endeavor. Imagine a world without hierarchy in place, a brain trust that allows for sharing a higher quantity of expansive ideas to generate better solutions, and that alone will create a world where there is the potential for everyone to have their own space.

Our educational system would be incredible if there were more diversified climates for learning, rather than rigid educational structures run by tenured administrators, worker bees who are loyal only to their union masters, and so-called educators who subsist on seniority rather than performance or inspiration, and then eventually the books are collected and prepared for burning.

Imagine the society we would have if the citizens who lived in it did not find their pocketbooks continuously raped by corporate middlemen, when they could be using that money on a needed surgery or life-saving treatment, and yet we are stockpiling outdated weaponry, when in reality we should be buying a weapon more powerful: the pen.

We have lost what used to make this society so revolutionary in thought, we don't even create the products we buy in our stores, every type of labor that exists is always outsourced, every politician has other people filling their wallet, because humans will never stop being filled with greed; there is not a single soul that can't be bought. The year we see on our calendars may change every three hundred and sixty-five days without a societal win, the system will turn into more paperwork we have to fill out every cycle, and things will never change unless we realize it's a critical climate we are currently living in.

Sick Society

Everyday the numbers grow, more and more people get diagnosed with medical problems, and the medical industry has nothing but profits to show. People are afraid to open their mailboxes because of the bills that reside inside, with this class system in place and insurance prices running high, there is nothing anyone can do about it; all they want to do is run and hide. The waiting rooms in hospitals are filled with people who have to wait in pain, it is first-come first-serve, and it's amazing that people are able to sustain.

Even when you are seen at the hospital you have to be near-death to get a bed, everyday more and more people are diagnosed with mental illnesses, and the only cure is more archaic pills for them to be fed. The pharmaceutical companies are only trying to cure the illnesses that the majority of the masses live; there is no concern over who is in the most pain, it is only about the people who have the most monetary compensation to give. People fight for jobs where they don't want to work; all because they need the health benefits as their only perk. The government only gives free health insurance to those who are unable to work; these people are forced to go on Disability and receive just enough money to survive, and the system will not change it will only smirk.

There are homeless people on the streets due to their medical conditions, they live the saddest lives any human can experience, and they receive no daily fruition. We live in a society of sociopaths, everyone is only concerned about their own well-being, and they refuse to pay higher taxes because they just don't want to do the societal math. We work hard for every dollar we earn, we slave over monetary compensation, so why in this nation would we want to create a system where everyone gets treated the same? Other countries have socialized medicine and they seem to be operating just fine, but in this land of capitalism what's yours is yours and what's mine is mine.

We turn our heads when we see someone who is truly ill, we would rather turn our heads, forget what we just saw, and go on with our lives as a corporate shill. We have the mentality, "I work hard for my money – why don't they just get a job." We have no desire to create a social safety net for those unlucky souls, for those who were dealt with flawed genetics, for those who developed an illness through no fault of their own, all because we all have our own personal goals. There needs to be a more compassionate mindset, because as fate will have it, you will reproduce and your children will have a terrible illness, and then you will be the one in financial ruin that has to mortgage your house just to pay the hospital debt.

Why not take this to the next level, set up "firing stations" on every block in every city, when people are too ill to persist they can just request from the government an end to all their pain, so they can terminate their life that has become grim and gritty. They can open the letter sealed from Uncle Sam, in it will be a 9mm bullet, and they can go to a "firing station," sit in the chair, put the bullet in the slot, and then they can snuff out their painful existence right there. More jobs will be created, we can instate a body removal crew, and this sick society will end and be dated.

Changing Classes

We love what we hate. We hate what we love. There's no one above us, so we just push and shove. We are living in a society with secretive sociopaths. No matter how you crunch the numbers, it is just flawed math. There are homeless people on the streets; there are people begging for help at our feet. We lack the empathy to care about anyone whom we don't personally know. We don't hold back as we deliver the final blow. Everyone's faces just blend into the crowd; if there is no personal gain, we just ignore them as we put on our shroud.

When money is our only objective, we are nothing more than a being who remains defective. We will backstab anyone who gets in our way; there is no black-and-white, only the color gray. We are slowly destroying this planet we live on; we are slowly marching toward the end of humanity, and soon enough, we will be gone. These are the end of times; the things we do to our environment are the ultimate crimes. The clock is ticking, but all we do is sit at our computers constantly clicking. Long ago there was a continent called Pangaea, but then the Earth changed and separated our lands – and now, just as the change in the tectonic plates, our economy divides us, and some of us can't even put food on our plates. Times have gotten so tough, people are starving to death; people are smoking meth; every minute, hundreds exhale their last breath.

Science can't save us because people hold it back; what will eventually kill us all is the empathy we lack. Love is an emotion that we are learning to forget; it's sad that we have evolved so far and now we have become our own biggest threat. What it boils down to is religion holding everyone back; it's because of our beliefs that send us in the mode to attack. How many more have to die, because we all can't seem to learn to see eye-to-eye? Everyone in every place in this world is secretly in pain; yet we are forced to put on a smile on our faces and claim we're only part of the food chain.

Animals are put to death because we have developed a taste for their flesh, when it's the human palate that needs to refresh. We have become so advanced that drones patrol our skies; if you defy the power, you are the one who dies. These are the ends of times, and nature will destroy us for our greedy ways and crimes.

Scientific Sorrows

Science often challenges the prudent confines of moderation, it infests our food supply with chemicals and free radicals with organic molestation, and it pollutes our organs and sources of oxygenation. Our bodies suffer as cells replicate, tissue bleeds, and acids boil within those vessels inside us, and it is the price to be paid in the name of generating greater wealth through efficiency and quantity; no more than monetary pus. When we alter the way things happen organically, it backfires on us in a way somewhat volcanically, and we destroy ourselves in a systematic process that is no more than mechanically.

Ways of resolving conflict become deadlier and more dangerous as we rely increasingly on metals and gaseous pockets, it turns drone warfare into a convenient solution, and it inflicts casualties by the flight of a manmade rocket. Satellites and sensors enable human swine to eavesdrop their way into positions of leverage, and foreign enemies use cyberspace to spew their vile propaganda at potential allies while they guzzle their opiated beverage.

The Internet can be used to reach out and connect in a meaningful way, but it can also be abused to deceive the uneducated with lies that have political sway. The days have died where people open the pages of a book, because people are content reading its text on an electronic screen; illuminated windows make it easier to look. Tales of gossip and greed are now considered headline-making news, and consumers are more worried about purchasing a new brand of shoes. Being told what to think by the moving-picture screen has supplanted actual human speech, and this is how we get our information by being a technological leech.

Then there are those who claim science holds the answers that religion fails to reveal, and this creates a new and twisted religion of their own that gains massive appeal. They remain confident that gods are fictitious, and anyone who believes otherwise suddenly lacks credibility and is suspicious. Their hyperbole rails against the inanity of a faith-based culture, yet it simultaneously depends on faith to justify its own framework like an overhead desert vulture. In their blind quest to expose the hypocrites who warp religion to control the masses, they also demonize those agnostic minds that see the value in questioning everything with rose-tinted glasses, and this includes theories and evidence taught in classes.

Corporate Companions

No matter how much we evolve, no matter how much we progress, no matter how much technology advances us, there is one instinctual trait that we will never deviate from, there will always be a trait engrained in us we couldn't solve. Together as humans we work as a team, we are naturally pack hunters; we accomplish whatever we need to survive and then when night falls, after we fill our needs we go off in a dream. The lone wolf that doesn't fit in with the pack lives the hardest life imaginable, because he has no comrades to help him organize his attack.

Only a certain percentage can be the dominant one, there is always one alpha male, and he rallies the other members, his fearsome attitude is only mimicked and none of his kin will ever run. There may be power struggles in the pack, the one with no fear of death will always remain on top, because the leader keeps the rest of the members alive, and because of this his power does not lack.

We as human beings act the same exact way, except in corporate America there is a structure built, there is an order to prevent a dominant uprising, so those with power inside them are forced into a job of repetitive tasks, and there is always the fear of losing all they have gained, so that fear makes them stay. You have to prove yourself in this organization; you have to have a perfect record that has no mistakes, you have to be a soldier that marches to the order of the corporation if you want to continue working in your station. You have to march to the beat of the slave driver's drum, you have to jump when you are told to, or it is the lone wolf who you will become.

Very few people say no to this system, they have a vision in their minds of a company that they feel will bring monetary fruition. They try to set up their own shop, hire workers that they feel are worthy, they don't run things like clockwork because they don't have knowledge of how to rise to the top. After a year of operation, they go through failed business attempts, screw-ups, and a machine that does not run flawlessly, they eventually have to fold and go bankrupt and they are overcome with deviation. This is the fate of the majority of all lone wolf start-up companies; they have a vision with unknown blind spots, with an incompetent crew operating it, and eventually the flame burns out, investors disappear, and they run out of money. The American nightmare at it's best, someone who thinks they are the alpha male with the greatest ideas, but after they put their dreams into motion they find out they are no better than any of the rest.

What it boils down to is the companionship of the flock that you lead, every person is a link in the chain that will break your company if weak, or you will be rewarded with success if you all succeed. A leader is no stronger than the people he hires; you want people willing to die for your vision if you really want to build a fire. One should look for an attitude of a loyal fanatic that will follow your every word; you want warriors who will sacrifice themselves for the greater good of the pack, you want strength in every aspect if you are going to properly lead the herd.

There is the person who is just looking for a paycheck and is not dedicated to the needs of the group, when stuff starts to get rough at work, which it will, these people are the first to fly the coop. Look past the sheet of paper they use to represent their past, look past the clothes they are currently presenting themselves with, look past the mask they are wearing at this moment; rather ask them a few questions that will help you determine if they are here for the moment, or if they are here to be a part of the pack and see if they are built to last.

Secretive Sociopaths

Narcissism is what someone experiences when stuck in a society that is only concerned about each individual. The narcissist will realize how their only chance for true survival is by caring about other people, and that is what is turning humanity into a society of secretive sociopaths. When you can't empathize with other individuals – remaining concerned only about yourself – you are actually slowly destroying yourself, because it is society that makes you who you are. We are still stuck in the mentality of the "survival of the fittest," when, in reality, the fittest won't survive – because we are all one. When we stop being a collective and just start being individuals, it slowly and gradually destroys those who are around us – and by proxy, whether one admits it or not, one's own soul. Slowly but surely, we are killing those with whom we come into contact – which is incredibly unfortunate, because we are actually just killing ourselves.

Radical Receptors

In the human body there are receptors that are just waiting patiently for the right molecule to come along so they can attach and bond, this concept goes beyond biochemistry as it can be applied to our society, because there are people out there waiting for the right waves of thought to come along; they will be attracted to these words and a friendship is founded; both parties will be mutually fond. It's how people find the right lover, it's how businessmen create partnerships, it's how musicians collaborate, it's how writers work together on a masterpiece, and it's how people come together; one is a receptor just waiting for the right entity for it to discover.

Everything that happens biologically in our bodies can be directly related to how our society functions, everything on a microscopic level happens in our daily lives, and it's how the world operates in junction. Keep your eyes open in the world you live in, there are people who are open receptors just waiting for the right person to come along, and if you are think freely and act the same you might just bump into someone who is your intellectual twin. Certain people don't mesh, they are not an open receptor, nor are they something you want to bond with, you are looking for a similar mind no matter the color of their flesh.

Travel into society blindly and with no fear, personify chaos in your activities, because this is the best way I have found to find the people you want to bond with and be near. Change your routine on a daily basis, don't do the same things that make you comfortable, always try something new, because if you continue doing the same things you will end up in stasis. Venture onward into the unknown and brandish your intellectual scepter, present your mindset and don't fear what other people may think of you, because you are just a molecule of society looking for the right person who is a receptor.

Inherit Intellectual

We are lonely and we wander around these different lands, with every possible mate who comes into our presence, they all have tiny flaws we pick out that we can't accept, and that just don't meet our demands. We are looking at the wrong things when we find a mate; we are looking at all the microscopic details, rather than looking at the big picture of how their brain operates. Do they have a nice car, do they have a house, and do they have a career that will take me far? These details are what end most relationships from the start, we are so zoomed in on the small details that makes someone who they are, and because of this social Darwinian trait it makes most eventually dart.

What we should be looking at are thought patterns and intellectual frequencies, the way people think and operate around logical problems, and if we paid more attention to this it would end in fewer break ups, fewer divorces, and fewer people would flee. It's the waves of thought that bind two beings of essence truly together, they become symbiotic in their relationship, and their existence will be something that transcends space and time into something eternally forever.

The people with low intelligence bind together over trivial things, they have common interests and they use them as building blocks for something that will eventually fail, they will fight back and fourth when their frequencies do not align, and eventually one of them will part ways from a relationship that goes back and fourth like a swing. There needs to be a shift in the paradigm of how lovers attract, they need to stop focusing on trivial details of material possessions, and most importantly they need to start paying attention to the way another will act.

People everywhere get married because they are lonely and they want a soul mate, when in reality these people are just acting on carnal desires of wanting to reproduce, and they get stuck with someone whom they on a daily basis have to tolerate. This leads many people stuck in marriages to have a wondering eye, they are stuck with someone with out the same intellectual frequency, and then they break their wedding vows and start to lie. They tell each other like empty husks that are forced to emit emotion, saying things at the end of sentences like, "I love you" when long ago it has vanished; the notion of devotion.

They will secretly go on dating websites in search for someone who can once again bring them felicity, in a life they have created filled with faux feelings, and even then when they cheat on their eternal lover, they find discover this new person is nothing more than a new fling, and in the end they are left with a marriage in shambles and insides filled with toxicity. It is the society we have created, in a capitalistic world of people choosing mates based on trivial facts and products, in later years people regret choosing that person with whom they mated.

What needs to change for this society to fix this problem that ails us, we need to stop looking at what people crave as consumer products, and we need to start looking at intellectual frequency rather than material objects that make us fuss. Start looking at the thoughts people say, start looking at the way people solve problems, start looking at people's vocabulary, and stop looking what their grocery cart looks like in a scornful way. We have become nothing more than individuals who are attached to the products that we so blindly follow; we are nothing more than corporate soldiers, and that has made us internally hollow.

Couples who are the happiest in life, those who truly can withstand any problem that surfaces are those on the same intellectual frequency, and these people can overcome any strife. Those who think alike have an internal bond so great that no spokesperson on television, no catchy radio commercial, or no cleverly-designed advertisement in a magazine can tear them apart. These people have melded minds that can beat anything life throws at them, and these are the same people who walk together to the grave, if you are lonely and stuck without a mate, keep searching through the dirt and in the end you will find someone with the same intellectual frequency, and in your heart they will be your eternal gem.

Societal Stigma

We are living in a land where our thoughts dictate how we treat one another, we are living in an archaic mindset, we are still racially divided, we are still sexually divided, and we are still divided by those who are sick; we live in a land where no man is our brother and no woman is our mother. We let the media tell us who to stay away from, we discard the homeless like it's nothing but their own doing, we veer away from drug addicts who are just trying to escape from the pain of existence, we drive different routes to avoid going into a slum. We are plagued by the concept of a cultural norm, we can't live in harmony, and we avoid people who don't resemble our characteristics or form.

We let religions divide us, we let the news stories skew our perception of living together, we live in fear of other people, and we as human beings have turned into no more than a wound that emits pus. We all have hearts, we all have brains, we all have different languages that we speak, so why can't we accept each other as human beings and begin a new age of acceptance, a clean slate, and a clean start? More and more people are becoming mentally ill, yet we fail to view it as an evolutionary trait; no, we walk away from them in fear because of the ignorance that is instilled. We look at people with different colors of skin, we use the stereotypes that poison the air we breathe, and we walk away from these people because they are not our kin.

We are bred to judge other people based off their circumstance, we cross the street when we see them to avoid contact, and we complete this evasion like the memorized steps of a dance. I have started to put an end to this ignorance in society, I will tell anyone I meet of my medical diagnoses both physical and mental, they are instantly disarmed from the emotional front they put up on a daily basis, and then the strangest thing happens, they tell me all of their troubles, we bond in variety.

The time has come to end us judging one another as beings, so start educating people you meet, make them realize you are the same type of creature, information is the key to unlock these past thousands of years of discrimination, teach them about what you experience, and that knowledge will not send them fleeing. We are in a society of uneducated sheep, start informing people about what we are becoming as a nation and end this societal stigma, if one person learns the life of another every day, than all this avoidance of what we as human beings really are will be put to sleep.

Trivial Time

Long ago, we were a group of dispersed, disparate tribes who roamed the lands. The only time we knew was the cycle of seasons. We watched these seasons change; we knew when it was time to plant crops, harvest our staples of food, and this was the only system we had. We were following the signs of Mother Earth to guide us in what to do, when to do it – and it made us survive.

As our society evolved, so did our intelligence; then, those who came into power devised a new way to keep us organized. These forces created a system that every man should follow; a universal system, on a universal scale, which had us all synchronized in a system that would only encourage and motivate us to progress on a day-to-day basis. We used to live in the now; we used to live from moment-to-moment – but then, once this system was incorporated into our mindset, people who used to be a tribe became indoctrinated into a society, a collective whole. Everyone was to follow this system, destroying any thoughts that would keep us in the moment.

We went from living in the moment to living in the minute, the hour, the month, the year, and the decade. Then, we indoctrinated everyone into the notion of a century. We put a time limit on everything we do as human beings: when we should be at work, when we should meet people, and it's something that hovers over us at every moment. "What time is it?"…"Will I be late?"…"I'd better hurry"…

You can't move at your own pace anymore; time is nothing but a constant race to constantly evolve, to constantly build, to constantly thrive, and to constantly survive. If you don't follow this notion of time, you will be left homeless on the streets – on the ground, and no longer on your feet. We have twelve months to try to better ourselves; we have anywhere from twenty-eight days to thirty-one days to make a paycheck, to keep us alive, to keep us buying material possessions we desire.

We have one day to go to work, do our daily chores, feed ourselves – and this time becomes stressful. It builds anxiety in our soul. We were initially programmed from the beginning to move at our own pace; but now, we have to be at a certain obligation to be at a certain place.

For me, I no longer follow the calendar: I don't follow months, I don't follow days, I don't follow hours, and I don't follow the minute. I don't know what time it is. I don't wear a watch; there are no clocks in my house. I live every moment in the now – and since I have adopted this notion, I get more done in a day than when I was following the system that has lasted for many millennia. But for most, that is considered the only way: to follow time. Time is a construct, a motivational tool for the masses; it helps keep us all synchronized on the same spectrum. It makes society function.

The clock is always ticking, forcing you onto a schedule; it will only leave you in a state of screaming and kicking. The masses still need to follow the time we have created, for it has helped us to progress this far as human beings. But there are some who don't need to follow time, because it is trivial – so try not to let time overwhelm you. Time is a waste of time; time can rob you of your life, and can be a crime; and, finally, those who are able to live in the now will blossom into their prime.

Statistically Superior

Those who hold political power over the masses will claim propaganda machines that control the three classes, and then things will suddenly change in front of your eyes; off come the rose-tinted glasses. When you have statistics behind your creed, you only begin to feel the greed, and that's when you feel your kind must lead; the rest in your way will bleed. Push them to the ghettos as you take to the streets, you have the power in Congress, because you have the seats; no paper trail and no receipts. Once the combined pigment of your brothers has the power, let the bells of your church deafen them from each tower, and then engineer the Zyklon B and turn on the shower; strip the gold off them as they cower.

The minorities will always be turned into a monetary slave, those who try to rebel will looked at as stupid and not brave, and slowly they will all be pushed to an unmarked grave; the force of power's tidal wave. Whether these people have the worst jobs that no one will want, the ones who rule over them will be nonchalant, and the history books will continue to haunt; power overwhelming can only flaunt. The media will always portray things as the beginning when it's the end, then when it becomes your waking reality you cannot pretend, and the damages that it will do to both people one will not comprehend; those once screwed will never turn into a best friend.

There will always be a demonization and mistreatment of those who have fewer numbers in the demographic, these people will have to heed to the powers of greater traffic, and deeds done to support them will only be viewed as pornographic.

Those who call themselves statistically superior, they generally live in lands exterior, and the ones stuck in the middle will be inferior;

survival off the plight of the interior. When the general consensus of the society that has power over the state remains most prominent; one will only act in a manner that is morbidly dominant.

Tainted Trust

Two of the most important qualities a human can possess are trustworthiness and a lack of fluctuation in their reputation, whenever a person earns someone's trust, their reputation becomes something that is undeniably enhanced, yet similarly it is something that is so delicate it can be destroyed for life by the actions of a single unannounced deviation. People will trust an individual by the praise of others, the trust of an entire crowd can be gained with one small action that causes others to make it something worthy of being spread by word-of-mouth, because it can turn someone with completely different political, scientific, and religious beliefs into their comrade and brother.

Trust is something that spreads faster than any virus among our society, everyone desires to follow those who they can trust because it is a survival instinct, it's because of this reason that we pick only a select few to trust, and not let in the garden variety. Our goal as a community should be the objective to elevate this kind of dynamic, as we should move our interlinking fabric towards greater depths of richness, only with the hopes to enhance trust within our universal multiplex, and because of this type of thought we will make someone's narrow mind into something quite panoramic.

Our greater objective here should be to propel this multiplex to a point where it can be a self-governing operation, we need to make it something that is based on the wealth of our interrelations, and we can kill this desire instilled in us from the very beginning to seek different of forms of continuous forms of validation. Is greed something that is in our internal programming in what makes someone a survivalist or a hoarder, will be able to wipe out that instinctual desire to have more than we need, and hopefully achieve the point where people can be trusted to create self-sustaining order?

It may be possible in a century of a constant conscious effort to do so on a grand level, we need to sidestep traditional government whether it be church or state, also we need to draw a clean line between organized religion and spirituality of man, because how can we fully open our hearts and accept one another if we think the actions of evil decisions are caused by the devil?

In our current technology we need a reliable and secure repository that is trusted by all, a safe vault of knowledge that will hold the data of everyone's reputations, and this will create a fail safe so this is not a society that we build to be to big that it inherently will fall. This will allow us to finally make no mistakes and no one that is a danger to others will wriggle through the nets, as we have a flawless system that will inform us who to trust, and this advancement to society will prevent us from inherently building up losses which makes everyone pay for the debt.

It is most cogent to base one's trust on actions and evidence of the past, rather than on faith alone, and this is a system that will make everything we build be manufactured to last. Trust and reputations are two sides of the same coin, if we could trust each other unconditionally, there would not be a need for a government to constantly police the streets, rather than leaving things that united us, things would change and together would join. The end result would be less corruption, less exploitation, and less waste, which, if it could work in one nation it would slowly spread to the others one-by-one, there would be no more tainted trust, and we would see the end of a certain type of person; the one who is two-faced.

The Collector, The Connecter, and The Defector

There are people in our society – a very rare percentage – who search for certain types of people. They are constantly seeking, constantly social-surfing…and they will not stop until they find themselves. They are looking for that human mirror. They are looking for souls who exist – mirror images of who they are.

These people think the same way, have the same intellect, have the same oddities, have the same troubles – and they are tired of dealing with the masses. They can't relate to normal people, because these people are not normal – they are the people who deviate from the norm, they are people who break the rules; they are the people who refuse to be used as societal tools. They have memorized every possible human conversation a human being can say to one another; they can manipulate any situation, and they are humanly personified deviation.

Without deviation, everything would constantly remain the same; nothing would ever change – we would never evolve, and we would only reduce our capacity for human beings to have a greater range. You collect what belongs with you, you collect to have someone understand you, you collect to have some companionship, and you collect so you have people to help you keep your grip.

You connect to unite people who think like you; you unite people who act like you; you unite people who know facts like you. You are the collector, you are the connector, you are the defector, you will not stop searching until the day you die.

You can spot them by the words they speak; you can spot them by their societal actions; you can pick them out of a crowd of one thousand people, and you convince them to join your faction. As a combined force you are unstoppable – you are all mentally-collected; a plethora of different husks with the same mind, you are a galvanized unified drive that will never again be rejected.

Line's Limits

Only a few members of our massive society walk the line; half the time it's brilliance, but half the time they are anything but fine. The parallel between what is considered amazing and insane is so similar it is almost inane. The insane dictate the new norms of the masses; the multitude of society following them like students listening to teachers in classes.

It is such a fine line to balance on; if you loose your footing, you are mentally gone. Some fall off that tightrope and never come back; but some manage a life of symmetry – those who have so much intelligence, they change the ruling order as they never look back. These people change the way you view the earth; they change the way you operate, and they give empty souls self-worth.

They operate on a level you can't even fathom; the answer of the universe is on their tongue – these people can be old, or, more astoundingly, incredibly young. They see through the lines that divide us all; they don't believe the lies that keep us in control. Intellectually, they are sprinting when you are just learning how to crawl. They have a higher consciousness, as they are looking at the big picture of our existence – while you are micromanaging every detail of your life from a distance.

With this gift comes a horrible price: a world of loneliness that no one can understand – you don't want this life, so don't even think twice. Most of these people never make it to see the intended end of their life; they opt out, unable to handle the pressure of something so immense – they choose to end it all, to escape this strife. They may change humanity for the better; they may end up institutionalized forever. It's all on how they walk the line; some can maintain, and some go in a downward spiral of nothing but decline. They walk the line.

Sand Society

There is a place in this world, a place where everyone can be free, a place where any mortal of logic and rational thinking shall truly be. My father owns a small town in the Mojave Desert – a town with no crime, no greed, and only pure freedom; one day, this place will be passed down to me. It is my birthright, and I will lead.

Everyone who follows the path of science can do what he or she desires – an intellectual community where all knowledge is universal; and with that foundation of truth, we will build a revolution in thought, as well as a complete empire. It is in the middle of nowhere, free from constrictions of the thoughts of the masses who still continue to live in the Dark Ages of time; in this place, there won't be a single prayer.

A place where all persons of reason and intellect – those with calculated minds – will be accepted, and, together, we will collect. The town is already solar-powered, so we are off-the-grid of fossil fuels; there will be no need for oils, and the climate is dry; not a man, woman, or child will worry about conflicting views as toils. Along with the solar power, we can begin to harness hydrogen and use that to power a new type of generation from within. The town has its own water supply that will never run dry. It is a self-sustainable community; no one will be greater than anyone else, and everyone will have the same opportunity.

This is the perfect place for a scientific revolution – where everyone is on the same wavelength. In this place that is a think tank for the rest of the world, there will not be any pollution. Many already know about this special place and the power that it holds, but there are many left whose power it does not behold. Let this message be a calling for all scientists alike, to gather en masse in this place – and the people who fear an overlord in the sky can take a hike.

This town must remain nameless for now; it is in California. If you look in the right places, you will find it with persistence. I am the last in line of my two brothers to control its existence. When I am given full control, we will grow our own food and resources; we will be a true democracy, where everyone votes on changes with a poll. It will be the beginning of a new scientific evolution, with everyone on the same page, on a daily basis; there will be no confusion. We will toil like clockwork everyday – each person doing what is required of them to enable them to stay.

The system will work, and it will not break down – with only people of high intelligence, compassion, and understanding, there will be no one in the darkness who will lurk. A pure community of only the enlightened: that is my vision, and we will no longer fear the unknown; we will no longer be frightened. This will be a global community of like-minded folks – I challenge you now to look up who the owner is of this place, look at the lineage of who will have this place in the future, and you will realize this is not just some message, not just some hoax. This is a calling, and together, we will help build a better society for people who live across the rest of the planet. It will be a logical land; all built by a people who are a society of sand.

DRUGS

Societal Sedation

The masses all moan in pain, for every person in every class, there is always an easy remedy that can be bought off opportunists, and when they get home with your stash you can finally tune out because you have something that you feel brings you some sort of gain. Crack is for the extremely poor who need a momentary way out, cocaine is for the rich who need an endorphin rush to make them feel momentarily empathetic, marijuana is for everyone who wishes to change one's perception from a dull reality to an interesting moment in time, opiates are for those who are in emotional pain and just cannot cope with the past, then there are hallucinogens that try to open up your third eye when you are too lazy to read a book, but in the end all of these will leave you empty inside; filled with no self-esteem and internal doubt.

Society turns to drugs because they're lacking affection, there is a common perception of the world that we all can see that is of unkind place where everyone suffers, in turn we abuse substances to escape from reality, because we would rather take the easy way out than be placed in a Governmental ordained section. The others turn to drugs as a way to escape the monotony and stress of the life that we are living, in the corporate machine that makes us lose our humanity, people would give anything to feel normal, and it is because of this desire that they view mental sedation is something more giving.

Then there are those who follow the examples set by other people they associate with, these individuals wish to emulate their role models or peers, and these opportunists and weak-minded individuals let them believe that drugs are the answer; that is the myth. Many of those who develop addictions do so because they have a family history of drug use, they see people whom they love using drugs and they will follow suit, and so they continue the gradual process of destroying their bodies and their minds; this is their war and they will not call a truce. Then come the groups of people that have a legitimate physical ailment, then they have doctors prescribe narcotics to cure their pain, that leads to the patient having an excuse to overmedicate, this will lead to an overdose which is a common loss of a brilliant soul, because this is the common pattern and tragedy behind our societal derailment.

Mental anguish and memories that cannot be forgotten, this is another factor that fosters one's dependence on drugs, because so many people go through life as victims of rape, violence, molestation, bullying, or constant criticism; substances that cure this momentarily cause them to go rotten. People feel that nothing they do is ever "right" or "good enough," they have such high standards to live up to, whether it be from the expectations of their parents, teachers, bosses, or even lovers, and this is why they always in the end choose to hit the good stuff. Nothing is ever as nice as the first high of any substance they take, people get locked in a predestined path that will lead them down the chemical rabbit hole, and then their habit of sustaining that feeling will drain every penny that they make.

Then lastly people turn to drugs because they are lacking fulfillment in their conscious realm, they wish for their lives to be more exciting, more meaningful, and to have a purpose, and they can't seem to find what they're looking for and they use drugs as a surrogate to fill that void; it is human nature to take the easy way out rather than to just overwhelm. No one likes monotony on any level of being, everyone desires a good dose of hedonism to ease the weight of the daily burden, we are just organisms which is why anyone can overindulge on pleasure, and when someone makes a habit of seeking out joy via a societal sedation; using is the bonding habit of a slave in lieu of a intelligent daily routine that is freeing.

Bottomless Beginnings

You watch in eager anticipation of her every movement she makes until she finally puts the plunger down. You will feel the warmth. No more frown. Drift away in your seat. It won't last long, so try to enjoy your treat. All that bitching and moaning just to feel the zone. Was it worth the wait? Are you enjoying your chemical date? It's like a mother's love, the laughter of a crowd, and a father who is proud. What you can't get out of life comes in a well-guarded clear cloud.

That's when the marathon starts. You chase after that feeling that you had just felt in your heart. Any amount of theatrics and verbal dialogue won't help you secure the golden frog that hides in that chemical bog. You think of every possible strategy to get that feeling back. Every thought becomes a plan of attack. Why can't you feel this love all the time? It becomes an endless ladder that you constantly climb.

Your ways of getting it to turn into something more devious, because every trick is more elaborate than the previous. People, dialogue, and circumstances just become hurdles in search for that touch. Eventually, you have danced in that garden of heat too much. Now, even the biggest dose won't give you that feeling. This whole cycle of trying to fill your soul with a chemical replacement is just for emotions that are locked in your mental basement. In the end, you are left high and dry, as nothing brings back that inner fire. Your body gets cold to the bone; just when you first started playing this game, you are all alone.

Opiated Options

The second that pill kick takes hold, the moment that plunger goes down it never gets old, and as it takes you away it breaks your mold; waves of pure inner warmth that you were sold. The weight is lifted that burdens your existence, the psychological pain that you ignore with persistence, and your tolerance may build with your consistence; lives of loved ones that get lost in your distance. It's your drug of choice because your reality requires sedation, you no longer feel the pain of life in your vacation, and this mistress will become your endless fixation; fuck the man who aided in your creation. Your speech will slur, your eyes will blur, and it is what you prefer; obligations that exist will defer.

It's a substance that makes you function in any task, when you are opiated you don't need a mask, while the rest of society drinks from a flask; when people see you they don't even need to ask. No matter your source of what makes you sustain, whether you pop it in your mouth or shoot it in your vein, because it makes every situation tolerable without a drain; the only thing that shuts off your never-ending brain. You may be a drug addict but you still can maintain, everyday that passes you lose your ability to refrain, and there is always going to be a reason that you will explain; the only thing on Earth that can cure your pain.

When you can't find a drug dealer who has what you need, you still need a source so it's a doctor whom you will mislead, that's when you learn everything you must say to succeed, and the lies that flood out of your mouth of phony ailments are like a stampede; all for another dose of what makes you feel freed. When the doctor whips out his prescription book you become a salivating dog, just so you can down them so quickly it could make your throat clog, and you can't wait to fill it at the pharmacy so you can get lost in the fog; the machine has made you no more than a cog. When the doctor finally has a reason to not believe your story, you have to surf for a new one that only kills your glory; just so you can resupply your personal inventory.

The day finally comes where you exhaust every possible way, you finally have to deal with sobriety that is here to stay, and that's when withdrawal becomes a state of decay; burned by the fire that now makes you pay. Your sensation of warmth is now nothing but cold, you sit under the shower until your water heater starts to withhold, and you quiver and shake; you can't uphold. Your opiated options created this path, every time you go down this road you will feel the wrath, because you just couldn't cope with your problems; eternally fearing your psychological math.

Operation Overdose

You become unable to tolerate the emotional pain of your existence, you just want out and there is no longer a desire for resistance, and so you make the conscious choice to go the distance. People simply do not care, keep your misery to yourself and do not personally declare, because you are nothing rare in the state of your despair. You are in debt up to your eyes, you can't even afford enough for daily supplies, and no one listens to your cries; a lonely existence with no allies. This is the only road that is left to take, whether it is poison in your veins from the snake, whether it is the noose around your neck that will not break, or the bottle of pills that will make you lifeless after a violent shake; to no longer want to be awake.

You turn your phone off and take the battery out, when you have done this in the past you tend to call your friends and shout, and this time there won't be paramedics having you chug charcoal as you pout; the end of the road without a doubt. You take two entire bottles of narcotics with acetaminophen to shut down your liver, you take an entire bottle of prescription sleeping pills so you won't quiver, and you get in the warm bath so you do not shiver; time to take away the life of the giver. To speed things along, you slit your wrists vertically with a razor blade, as you slowly bleed into the tub you eyes begin to fade, and this is how your last card is played.

Your heart will begin to overload from all of the pills, it will start to beat erratically and give you the chills, because you took enough for all of Beverly Hills. Your lungs will slowly fill up with less and less air, you will have trouble breathing with both of the pair, and you will be so high you hardly seem there; the noose is waiting by the chair. Your body is rejecting such a poisonous combination, your mouth goes dry and there is no salivation, and you can barley move from all the sedation; the brutal end for a percentage of the nation.

This is your sixth time trying to finally put your body to rest, looking back the other times just seemed like just a test, and this time you did everything right; you did your very best. Most people would just die in that little room, it's not that easy for you though, because you will just wake up the next day in pain and gloom. Your body is resilient which prevents your doom. The failure that was your operation overdose, you tried your very hardest and you came very close, and you ache everywhere and feel nothing but gross; some cannot die which is an existence quite morose.

"Why does the truth in our lives change on a daily basis? Are we are all so emotionally flattened from the reality of our nature; the only way to break stasis?"

"Evil was good, but then it started lying."

"The streets of gold are paved with the flesh of the ones who never get stuck in a mentality of old, because they always break the mold; they are forever bold."

THREE

LANDS OF CONSUMERISM DICTATE YOUR ASSOCIATIONS WITHIN THREE CLASSES, BECAUSE ETHNICITY IS SIMLY A SHROUD THAT NOTIONS STATISTICAL PERCEPTIONS OF YOUR EXISTENCE TO THE MASSES; A PYRAMID-LIKE SYSTEM THAT THOSE DEEMED WORTHY GET THE GREENER GRASSES...

"A gift to those who can appreciate something is a curse to those that convey it."

"Politicians are actors who manipulate words to gain popularity, and once they have the approval of the majority; they abuse power in corporate interest in our society."

"Wars create times of peace, and then pieces of time create wars."

EARTH

Moss on the Rock

We are the perfect distance from the sun; it provides us with heat, makes plants photosynthesize, which provides us oxygen to breathe. A perfect distance that makes every living organism's heart beat. It is not close enough to burn everything on the land; we are just far enough away to grow life, just far enough to make everything stand. If it were too close to us, nothing on this Earth would exist; it is the power that puts every inhabitable organism on the list.

Instead, a miracle happens; warmth goes far enough to provide life – and it burns for so long, it gives us time to evolve into something that's eventually so globally divided all we experience is strife. We started out as one continent, just like everything evolved; Earth shifted from Pangaea, to multiple different landmasses – and because of that, our mentality of unity dissolved.

We, as humans, act like a superior species; we dominate other animals like a commodity – we are the force that is slowly destroying ourselves, which is a bizarre fucking oddity. What virus willingly destroys the environment that sustains it? It's people with one thing on their minds: power and control – they will never quit. We will eventually destroy this place that is so special; everyday, more and more species go extinct – and everyday, more and more criminals end up in the police precinct.

We are moss, growing on a rock in outer space; there is nothing in this universe like us. There is no other intelligent existence, and this is the only place like this; but what brings tears to my eyes is how there's no resistance. How long can we fight over fossil fuels – that we will inevitably run out of? How long will we kill each other over trivial divisionary borders? When will we realize that what is going on in this planet is the most special thing in the universe? When will we realize that every single action we take is nothing but perverse?

We evolved from an evolutionary soup of the right amount of chaotic chemicals when an asteroid exploded over our sky. Will we have evolved into something that will only evolve to die? It's sad that there are so many of us living as barbarians – when we really should be nothing but humanitarians. We don't have long to fix our sick habits: from the plastic that is collecting in the ocean, to the oil that is spilled on a monthly basis – try to maintain damage control all you wish.

Let the media make you believe that everything is okay –

because, in the future, we will look back at the damage we have done and it will do only one thing: haunt us. The moss may grow on this spinning rock in the cosmos, but time is a critical factor – and our decisions should be based on more than which politician is one's favorite actor.

Constant Conflict

Human beings love conflict. It is in our nature, it is engrained in our DNA, and it is a part of us in every way. We have been fighting to survive on this planet for so long that we don't even recognize times of peace anymore. It's all about amassing weapons for the next great conflict. We thrive, we grow, we arm, we go, we kill, we fight, and we can no longer see right. We die, we cry, we surrender, and we pray, but this will keep going on and on, everyday.

Borders divide us, countries collide us, and no one wants to stop, because it's just how you grow the crop. We are all in pain, everyday, and there's always someone there to take it away. It's the flow of the tide, it's the way we march and stride; it's the way we don't look at each other with love in our eyes, it's the way we believe each other's lies. We act like such friendly neighbors, until we feel the endless labor; then we snap, we murder each other, and it's life's giant mousetrap – we are no longer sister or brother.

Families break apart, friends dissipate, lovers disappear in the night, and the only emotion we are left with is boiling hate. We have forgotten what makes this world such a beautiful place, which is the innocent look on a child's face. We have forgotten how we need to touch each other and hold hands, because that's the only thing that will save all of our divided lands. The simplest thing, a gesture, and a smile, someone who lets the doves go to open their wings, can transmit love. Every night we all go to bed drowned in sadness, because we are surrounded by such madness.

Every form of media just shows how we are broken and ill, and we all just want to swallow that pill. The way we heal as a people is just to stifle our inner trouble, and there is only so much we can take as individuals before we pop our own bubble. We are all lost, following false figures who promise to heal us; when, in reality, the ones who can are the ones who are near us. If we all just stood arm-in-arm, and felt what it was like to be a tribe – just like how we all started, not one of us would break the circle to take a bribe.

The money that motivates us to do everything wrong, is why

so many need to join together and sing a song. The melody will be nothing but peace, as we all stand in silence and no one will need the police. While I was in the hospital, a nurse held my hand because she knew I was in pain; she wouldn't let go, and I tried to pull back and refrain. After a few moments that passed, I accepted her healing touch, and then I felt like I could last.

Just that mending affect, which she intended to be direct, made me forget about fighting the pain, and I felt I could just sustain. That's all it took. The love of a stranger with compassion in her eyes, to make me realize that the clouds have lifted and I was staring at open skies. We forget as human beings that we can have a healing touch – and sometimes to make the affliction vanish, we don't have to do much. We have to open something that we have never used to succeed, which is dropping our arms, forgetting about greed, and showing that some of us are not capable of harm.

Once these people of peace and intelligence start to rally, they will turn the world into something more than a death toll tally. Fight your instinct to hate, and just let that emotion disintegrate; feel a new emotion that you couldn't feel but knew was there the whole time, feel peace in your heart with human compassion and you will forget that phrase that plagues us called the "victimless crime."

Power's Potential

We all yearn for it, we shill for it, we burn for it, and we all kill for it. It's the dividing line between territorial borders, and it's the current world order. Like an engine that pulls a train, it is a source that will tap right into your vein, and from it you will only try to gain, but in reality it's the main source of all your pain. We strive for it, we lie for it, we thrive for it, and we so desperately cry for it. Just as the Earth orbits the Sun, just as the police officer holds his gun, just as the hound dogs have their fun, and just as every guilty man will always run.

It swills us, it consumes every part of us, it thrills us, and every time it exhumes us. It is the man chopping down the ancient tree, it is the desire to destroy every flea, it is the rapist thrusting with sadistic glee, and it is the source that bonds all of us in chains; preventing us from being free. It fills every part of us, and it fakes us, it chills us, and then it unfortunately breaks us. A chain running the Earth, we all search for it from our birth, it turns sadness into mirth, and its inner fire warms your girth.

We purr for it, we pry for it, our visions blur from it, and we all vie for it. It's the blank check that you write; it's the bloodlust that you fight, hitting bone with all your might, and the fact that you always have to be right. We strive for it, we adjourn for it, we drive for it, and we sadly every time will turn for it. It's what we arrogantly gauge, it's that rather pungent taste of sage, it's your egotism spewed in rage, and finally it's the hand that will slam your cage.

Creating Cures

The cure is something so simple, and something so pure. Humanity will begin to heal once it has the person who will lead us to intellectual salvation; humanity will begin to heal once it realizes there is no damnation. We cause our own fate, and what leads us down the path of darkness is the feeling of hate. Once we begin to love each other as one, together we can accomplish anything, and anything will be done.

Awakening Apathy

From the day that you end a lifelong lie, you end your fear of an overlord watching over you, and abolish your need for a security blanket that lives in the sky. All those years you lived without fear, everything would always turn out great no matter the circumstance, and nothing bad would ever happen; you would never shed a tear. As you gained in maturity and intellect, the science you learned in school would only contradict your childhood fairytale, and you would grow up only to defect. Corruption in every land, children being molested, and starving people would die daily, as no one would extend a giving hand.

It's these things that others push out of their minds, they wanted to pretend everything was safe and happy in their police state that is a candy-coated dictatorship of a democracy, and we push the souls who suffer out of our minds, they live a hellish existence in another land, we get caught up in the latest fashions, the newest electronic devices, and a fancy new car to drive, we so desire this consumer-based place, the last thing we would ever think about is those who are in a struggle to live, because who wants to think about their turmoil and daily bind?

Even things at home where everything is supposed to be safe, things are anything but pleasant, the mentally ill grow in numbers every day and the pharmaceuticals make customers not cures, and the lower classes fear to open their mailboxes because the very next medical bill could push them past that financial mark of destitute making them a modern-day peasant. People are armed to the teeth, because everyone has a survivalist mentality filled with paranoia, everyone is prepared for a revolution, which will never happen so just let your bayonet rust and leave it in your sheath. The power that runs lands established by freedom on every level, with each passing day more and more control is forced on our society, and when I see the homeless trying to survive on the streets they look like they are in hell, but I see no devil.

There is no point in fighting anymore, it is an unbeatable system that is run by pure greed, everyone has their hands open, no pure soul ever gets into power and because of that we will not succeed. We created our doom and it was our own desire, we bought into material possessions and we became the dealer, the user, the addict and the liar. Everyone is stuck in jobs they don't want to do, we wear different masks for different people, and since we sell out every essence of our being we have lost our identity, and when we look in the mirror we no longer see ourselves, we gaze at ourselves in a puzzled manner trying to remember the person we used to be – "Who?"

Slavery still exists, but they no longer use chains, we our bound by our credit cards, and that stifles our desire to revolt because we must feed ourselves and we must sustain. The only choices we make in life are so pointless and trivial, we are past the time when one man had strength and his actions could do something extremely pivotal. How could you not wake up in this day and age and have the feeling of impending doom, day-in and day-out we tune into idiotic things that give us remote moments of pleasure; how could you not end up a statistic, who ends it all with a nine-millimeter bullet, just to escape the monotonous never-ending gloom. In this time of awaking apathy there are only few who can see the truth of this existence we have created, but sadly there are not enough of us to change the world; those people end up being only you and me.

Apathetic Apex

As the millennia roll over into a new age, our technological advancements have failed to advance our capacity for self-sufficiency, and we still find it acceptable as a society to move to the next page. We cruise down the street in fuel-guzzling, dirt-spewing, and environmentally-unfriendly machines rather than embarking on a leisurely stroll, and we blindly act like this will take no evolutionary toll. We are content with sending that email rather than writing out a letter, and we pretend that our psychiatric medicine actually makes us operate better. Even that step forward in technology known as the telephone call has been replaced by an impersonal text message, and we act like this depersonalization via communication is enhancing of our Humanity's presage.

Everyday individuals are embracing apathy in every step they make, it is always easier to dissociate and ignore living things around us as we selfishly chose not to give, but rather what we desire to take. These are the people who will vote for a political candidate because the media sways their favor, the people who push family members whom they don't want to talk to themselves to see a psychiatrist or therapist, and the people who buy a bag of processed food because they are addicted to the artificial flavor. The fat of the land interbreeds with the laziness of one's hand, and they choose to tune out to rest of the world to their idiotic mainstream music that is somehow labeled as a band.

This personal apathy emanates outward, as it spreads like wildfire throughout the daily routines of our cities and towns, and it only drives us as a whole in one direction; downward. People turn their heads the other way when they see an injured pedestrian collapsing onto the sidewalk, and they show no emotion as the police outline a body with chalk. They metaphorically jam their fingers in their ears when hearing words of prejudice flow from the lips of their fellow bourgeois, when they tune out the verbal hate speech no one is hurt, because all they can see is a flapping jaw.

In the end we should not expect the masses to show emotions, when we are neglected by the very government tasked with caring for us, we wonder why politics never change, because we are all just humans running through the motions. Those who spend more money on their political ambitions, when they could be feeding the hungry, educating the young, or safeguarding the biosphere, and this is how we choose to cope with these apathetic conditions. They are those who raid public resources to satisfy their own desires, confident that their antics will never be revealed, and they are the one who create the heat that burns us with their fires. When authority figures fail, so do those over whom they lord their domain, and they are the ones who we are following to pave the trail.

Simplified System

Obsessive over-complications in a wasteful society, we waste things that are still good, and we make things obsolete because they are not the newest fashion, but when will there be a time for environmental sobriety? People on food stamps barely have enough to sustain, middle-class families throw away half-eaten meals, the homeless must wait in line for food with no dietary value, and all because of our class systems in place that prevent all men and women from getting the equal nutrition for them to sustain. Over-consumerism is only worried about money to gain, pharmaceutical companies are only worried about repeat business, insurance companies only cover people with non-preexisting ailments; which only causes the masses with empty wallets to feel nothing but pain.

There is technology that is being held back intentionally,

environmentally-friendly fuel-efficient vehicles, massive solar power grids that would reduce pollution; if we only incorporated logical systems that would be something of a standard and something conventionally. Plastic that is collected in massive quadrants within our oceans, oil spills that wreak heavy damage on delicate wildlife, an ozone layer growing so thin it causes the polar ice caps to melt, can someone please tell me why there are not people on the streets causing an environmental commotion? Common household items that break should be fixed in an inexpensive manner, cellular phones that are replaced just because the new model is out, gas-guzzling trucks that are still purchased when no one uses them for moving purposes; is it so hard to resist the consumerism that plagues these lands, is it so hard for you to just be happy with what you have; to write down those things you absolutely need, stop being so impulsive, and only consume things when it's dictated by your day planner?

We need to be more environmentally thoughtful; we need to recycle on a weekly basis, we need to conserve the resources we have on this limited Earth, and finally we need to grab our own weight in this apathetic society, and grab our share of waste to be disposed; only to the garbage receptacles that we should pull.

Societal symbiosis should be the next part of the plan, no more judging people on race, religion, creed, and sexual preference, we should all be unified in harmony in a system where we work together, and, statistically, that will increase everyone's lifespan. Lastly, for a better society we need a security blanket in place for those who are unable to find independence on their own, the mentally ill who cannot fit into the daily workforce of all Americans, the elderly who have served long lives as good tax-paying citizens, and if we fix all of these maladies in our society then the numbers will reduce for the people with rebellion on their minds, and they will no longer be able to groan.

Morbid Morality

Most wars that occur are not about protecting our land of opportunity, they are about a never-ending mentality to dominate other lands and cultures, when the whole time we are profiteering off of natural resources, and the media only dictates that it is in the best interest of our community. Humans threaten to murder the loved ones who dare defend themselves of any of their enemies, they will destroy their cities and homes, and they will cripple their barely functional economies. Most instigators of war don't care how many hundreds of thousands of lives they destroy in their conquest for greed, they only see the neon lights of power and wealth on the horizon, this only drives them to subjugate others regardless of how much blood and rubble is left in their wake, they do it all without shedding a tear, because in the end they feel it is for the betterment of their own creed.

These Machiavellian quests end up producing human pain, their strife places a burden on the economies of rival nations, which takes its toll on the global economy, this is the cycle that proceeds to never to cease, because we disassociate the screams all for power that we gain. We pretend we are doing the right thing for the nation we call our home, the evisceration of other people's lives is a morbid practice, we have turned into creatures that promote genocide, torture, and destitution in the name of nationalistic and patriotic revolution, with these ideal, slogans, and propaganda we spread; there is no land that we don't roam. Political conservatives rail against the immortality of sex and violence in the media, then they turn right around and promote a relentless "National Security" campaign as part of their political agenda, these monstrous men sacrifice our good nation filled with a majority of whom only want peace, and because of the Internet they can no longer do the old practice of covering their deeds; rewriting the encyclopedia.

Too many people live by the old clichés of "the ends justify the means" or "to the victors go the spoils," if they feel they've come out on top at the end of the war, because a victory allows them to overlook how much blood washes over the soil. History has shown that those who are conquered will eventually revolt against their masters, old tyrants are replaced by new stealthy methods of rebellion that take place in the night, then the vicious cycle can continue to feed itself, and that is the cyclical pattern that is worse than any of our natural disasters. Absolute power serves no purpose in these modern times, other than to give the so-called victor an inflated sense of self-entitlement while causing misery, and somehow those who make these conflicts allowable will sleep fine at night; despite their war crimes.

What we have here is a society unlike any other that has existed, if we all finally stopped using war as a crutch, the system would inevitably change if we stopped letting our past actions dictate our future ones, and if we all initiated a global example of how to make the world a better, peaceful, and safer place to live; things would certainly become less twisted. Rather than coercing and manipulating the ones worthy of the label of our rival, we could start making attempts to relate to them and reason with them, then when people of our nation travel the world for pleasure that we won't be looked at as oppressors, and for once they will be happily greeting us upon our arrival.

Instead of obsessing over the next thing to go out and buy, when we really just need to appreciate what we have, if we fought this instinctual urge to always have more power, possessions, and trivial merchandise to fill our homes, because in the end we cannot keep things after we die. When nations and cultures began to cooperate and pool resources with unifying hands, rather than trying to steal them from each other, one could finally regard his onetime enemy as his global brother, then finally this morbid morality that exists won't plague the mindsets of the leaders, and that is when we can start joining territorial borders in all of the adjoining lands.

Demising Doom

As we evolve as human beings, in this fast-paced world filled with constant technological advancements, everything is gradually speeding up day-by-day, more and more of us are blinded by the speed of society, which unfortunately blinds us from what is important, and it prevents us from truly seeing. Our jobs demand more out of us every day, we try and compete with coworkers for a better position, we work ourselves to the bone, and we do it all for one thing, which is better pay.

We see our families less and less, corporations rob us from what should be important, we suffer so we can put adequate food on the table for our loved ones, we have no time for ourselves, and we can't seem to strive hard enough to fix our daily mess. Because of all of these stipulations in our daily lives, we experience one thing every day, with anxiety pills prescribed to nearly everyone who can't handle the stress, which is why we feel impending doom and every ounce of it hinders our drives.

We barely find things in this society to make us happy, most of us turn to drugs to escape the reality, the others commit domestic violence because they can't cope in life with their inability to provide, the only people who pretend to be blessed recite archaic things from an ancient book, and the majority cannot relate to verses so incredibly sappy. We wake up in our beds after the alarm goes off, we start to dread the day we will have to repeat over again like a human machine, the ones who can't go on with this routine take the easy way out, and others only call them cowards as they look at them as lesser beings while they comment and scoff.

Things have hit a breaking point where people simply cannot maintain, nearly everyone has been to the mental hospital, placed on meds that don't fix the situation, and this is the only thing society provides us with to give us strength to maintain. The demand of our workloads increases everyday, no matter where you work the stress is unbearable at times, and you can't complain about it because the economy is so bad this is where you are forced to stay.

Some people turn to religion to seek a happier existence, even in a place of worship where people are spiritually healed, the collection plate is passed around and everyone watches those who don't contribute, they are met with scornful looks and negative comments under the breaths of the flock, because even in the house of the holy if you don't contribute you are left with people who can't feel your despair and you are met with resistance.

How could one not feel they are trapped in a system of despair, from every angle and every organization of society, everyone has so many problems of their own it is anomaly when someone lends a helping hand and offers an ounce of human care. With the majority of people who have some sort of medical sickness, people are afraid to leave their homes to check their mailboxes for medical bills that pile high, in this land it is the survival of the class system in place, and it you want to save yourself from being homeless you have to act at any opportunity that presents itself with extreme quickness.

Our schools don't teach kids how to succeed on the outside, it is left to the parents to make sure their offspring find a good education, the teachers make less money each year, how are they supposed to develop young minds to be the people of the future, because the educators themselves to survive need a financial guide? Fear of the unknown makes everyone want to cower, we are in rocky times that are barely sustainable, and the lower two classes which are the majority hold none of the power.

Things that are supposed to inspire us to make the world a

more beautiful place, even art is just a business now, and the people with the true talent go unrecognized because they can't afford an agent to promote their face. It's no wonder people have a hard time coping with a day-to-day routine, we are all just replaceable cogs outsourced from other countries, and it makes this anxiety-inducing thing operate that is the current American machine. The impending doom will get worse each year, brace yourself for impact, things are beginning to fall apart, and these times have already become your biggest fear.

Fire Factory

From the second that lightening hit that first tree; from the moment we rubbed two sticks together to create that burning amber, at the first sight of it scared us and would make most flee. One needs two elements to survive as a human being, fresh water because that is what a majority of our bodies are made of, and oxygen to fill our lungs with air, so our brain isn't deprived of oxygen, which keeps us conscious and seeing. Once we evolved opposable thumbs the only other element we needed to succeed as a thriving race was the element of fire, and once we harnessed it's power it was the only ingredient we needed to evolve from just land dwellers to beings that would build empire after empire.

It all started with a spark, and soon we would use it to give us warmth in the winter, its heat would cook our food to prevent us from being sick, and it would provide us light from when times would get dark. As we grew more intelligent we learned that it could turn earthly materials into tools crafted from the right amount of heat it provided, we developed weapons that would make us unite into armies, we forged weapons specifically designed to kill, while the masses settled for more primitive tools that made every fight a slaughter and one-sided.

We went from tribes trying to survive in the wild, to men listening to those who had the power that ruled over the land, to barbarians who would rape and pillage, and it brought out a spirit in us that was dominant and riled. Then came the invention of the cannon, when that fuse was ignited with a flame, out blasted a ball that would destroy men, warriors in armor, and even stone structures, and that only started an arms race that would do more than just maim. Fire evolved into firepower, and any weaponless spirit would obey any command while they would cower. Then came the next evolution of warfare, something that any soldier could hold, the handheld rifle aimed at whomever one wanted dead; any man, woman, or child had this power to behold.

Now we needed something that could fire multiple shots at once, to pulverize many targets, the repeater was created, and intelligence or skill was not needed anymore for combat, anyone could blast off several rounds – even the dunce. The power of fire was harnessed in the pistol, from six rounds, to the reloadable clip, one could even dual-wield these weapons, carrying one on each hip. The advancements came one after the other, until the carbine, and then eventually the assault rifle came about, killing any who opposed your faction – even someone who was a mother.

Then Kalashnikov created the prize of his nation, something with a bullet of size that could kill nearly anything, with thirty rounds easily manufactured by a machine, and it would soon be mass-marketed to every third-world country that desired genocide; it was the currency of death, sending anyone without one to the end of their duration. The evolution continued along this path and they developed a seventy-five round drum, now just one person could take out an entire village, an entire ghetto, and an entire slum.

The bullet goes from the clip into the chamber, the trigger is pulled, and the firing pin strikes that special spot causing a micro-explosion, which sends the bullet speeding out of the barrel straight into the flesh, and after one bleeds out, then starts the process of the body's erosion. The rebirth after forest fire is ten times greater than when those flames consumed all those trees, but there is no rebirth after a bullet is fired, it only brings human beings to their knees. Is this the evolutionary process of intelligent, rational beings of higher thought, or is it war after war that should be fought?

Sadistic Silence

When engaging in a conflict with another soul, the cruelest thing one can do is by stop talking to them in whole, yelling back means you respect your rival enough to give them an explanation which could make them console, but only silence means your rival doesn't even warrant the energy to communicate with them that is a method of control. If people think he is too crazy to even acknowledge or speak to, his brain will torment him with ongoing paranoia that will stick like glue, and that is all he will ever hear for the rest of his life is more silence and madness will ensue.

Social interaction keeps people full of life, vigor, and purpose, to name a few, but the problem with life as an island is that you will eventually sink into the ocean without a proverbial social canoe. A person isolated from any other forms for them to sustain, they will ultimately proceed to neglect themselves just like the weakest link in the chain, they will hear the only the sounds of the echoes of their own voice and they will start to go insane, and then feel the increasing temptation to snuff out the lives of others just for attention to gain.

When people feel ignored they rail against anyone in their vicinity, they lash out at their elected leader for whom they may have once had an affinity, they might berate their well-meaning family members with physical threats proving masculinity, or castigate those whom they envy with a hatred that goes on for infinity. Their lack of desire to connect makes them appear mentally unhealthy, causing passers-by to avoid them altogether in a manner that's somewhat stealthy, or to report them to the proper authorities because they are not socially wealthy. Sadistic silence can be equivocated to physical abuse, you are punishing someone by ignoring that they exist which makes them feel like a social recluse, and if you are the type of person who uses this sadistic form of revenge – do the population a favor, and don't reproduce.

Devastating Devotion

We are all trapped in a culture where expressing the reality around us is unacceptable in every way, in this society loving the truth is the biggest sin imaginable, and because of the ones who keep us silent we have to bite our tongues every day. The sociopaths in control of this vast land that could be filled with endless hope, they have an enormous amount invested in their web of self-supporting lies, all which convince us to devote ourselves to the ultimate fallacy that love of money is the only thing worthy, because of this we will never be filled with true happiness, and we will drag our feet to every destination where we are required to go as we can only seem to mope.

Being awake to a single one of these lies makes one an eager seeker after the truth, the edifice of every lie that crumbles for those that are seekers, and the sad thing is that we were brainwashed with this false thinking from the days of our youth. One cannot wake up someone who is pretending to be asleep, the edifice of lies takes an effort of will to believe, or to constantly pretend to believe, all for the sake of an easy life, because of this reason the masses will always be happy as sheep.

The problem is not in waking people up to the truth, the problem is creating a society, here on this global consciousness at our fingertips and in real life, at a grassroots level, where love and truth are valued above all else, the answers are already out there, and it does not take the perception of a sleuth. The dilemma can be simply solved by saying "Hello" with a polite tone, you have two ears but only one mouth, so listen more to your fellow man at your side, because a community is built upon listening much more than talking, and the last thing we ever need is to walk into the bank because of our materialistic desires and ask for a loan.

Brother's Barrage

Together, we are an unstoppable force; sometimes I talk and the words are straight from your source. Something that burns inside of you is now a part of me; you have turned on something inside me that is pure power; when you command, others cower. You are the protector, I am the freedom fighter; you are the defector,

I am the gasoline and you are the lighter.

Together we have the ability to change those who are in pain, and we will do it selflessly for no personal gain. Fate brought us together in such a hellish place, and you are impossible to replace. Every time we sync up, I get inspired, we travel on the same wavelength; I was so weak, but you gave me the strength. You taught a dead man how to love; you made me see the light above. The age of fear is now at the end; I am the alpha, you are the omega – together, we will transcend.

AUTHORITY

Political Poison

Politics are synonymous with societal toxicity, factions of law are power-driven systems that involve greed and egoism through publicity, and they are deigned to take powers away from the ignorant with the utmost simplicity. Those selfish desires only exploit and cripple innocent bystanders who happen to be in the way, nothing positive arises from the manipulation and nastiness generated when someone works the system to capitalize on another person's misery without delay, and the actors who have won your favor through the media on speak the truth when the camera is rolling and it is time to display.

Family dynasties are the cornerstone of unhealthiness that is political, parents push their grown children into following in their footsteps causing offspring to make careers out of being abrasive and analytical, and they grow to be confrontational to preserve the family name they think is critical. Relatives show favoritism breeding resentment amongst the outcasts of their blood, if someone is different it intrudes upon the family structure like a flood, and it upsets the balance orchestrated by those patriarchs and matriarchs who seek to perpetually rule their roosts grown in financial mud.

Organizations embody many of the worst features of political machines, they are without the tangible benefits to their participants by any means, and generally power is dictated by the coding of one's genes. A fraternal order is supposedly based on camaraderie and respect, but it generally devolves into a sandbox fight when its members crave reverence or prestige that is the ultimate defect. Academic assemblies use verbosity and accomplishment to quantify their power, congregations of worship form hierarchies that determine the pecking orders within their social structures that make others cower, and if enough participants tire of such antics these groups will fade and die at the determining hour.

Our entire government is built upon a foundation of lies and oaths being rewarded with wealth and spoils, politicos desire upscale lifestyles for their own loved one who never toils, and so they neglect the needs of lower classes in order to achieve that end – all for overseas oils. They use the bully pulpit to actually strong-arm weaker men, they feign indignation or obliviousness when called on their actions time and time again, and they cover their nefarious actions with a prayer that ends in amen. Citizens justify bad behavior from their heroes by uttering the common phrases "All politicians lie" or "We cannot change the political system," no one is ever punished rather rewarded with media-based praises, and so this tainted beast thrives as a matter of self-fulfilling prophecy that reoccurs in cyclical phases.

Tragic Tears

Life in a world dictated by chance, chaos, and unpredictable elements can often be tragic, when things take a turn for the worse, events can produce a worst-case scenario, generally there is nothing we can do to fix these events that unfold, because there is no undo button and there is no magic. The true tragedy about human nature is we do not see all life as equal; we do not grieve a distant warrior as we would our kin, because this existence can often be painful; what makes it worse is there is no redeeming sequel.

The tragedy is a social sort, it is individuals who pay the price, and the solution is to encourage spirituality, kindness, and equality; there is no fix for when everything goes wrong, because there is nothing that lets you abort. The solution is not empty words in legislation, it is in our day-to-day activities, we have to stop seeing each other as trees in a forest, but rather take the time to value the unique individuals in our lives, because we should all accept we are only here for a short duration.

Knowing that by extension, believing we are all the same in our uniqueness, we can properly feel the death on a battlefield, coming to the final realization that every being, rich or poor, popular or alone, happy or sad, should be recognized; something worth a mention. Tears fall from our cheeks, people are treated differently because of the class they were born into, some people get to see everything the world has to offer, and some people don't even get a peak. Divisions among beings who all have the same skeletal structure, beings who have the same organs that make us operational, flesh that may have different tones of color, a brain that has the same power to operate in every soul, sadly we keep ourselves in separation, because that is the design of our segregated infrastructure.

Our pride, selfishness, and greed prevent us from complete unification and halter us from growth, we can never all agree on one thing that will make these tragedies end, we innately want everything that we admire, what about equality and kindness, are we so bent on what makes us filled with desire that we can't have both?

This is why we have tragic tears, this is why things will be this way forever, because of the way things are it is pointless that we still even count the years.

Emotion Engineers

Emotions resemble piano keys in that when you push them in different combinations you will get a unique serenade of music each time, just like how a supposed friend says things to make you feel guilty in order to coerce you into completing a specific task that does not pay a dime. A hot-tempered lover uses saccharine platitudes to invoke their desired sexual position, and the toxic colleague passively criticizes your work that drives you to second-guess your own judgment or competence with suspicion. Words invoke a buffet of sensations that fuel the way we choose to treat one another, because if it's in your favor why not call the guy who is your next meal ticket your brother?

Some people use these tactics to transcend an interpersonal relationship and affect a social cluster, friendships breed cliques and they isolate you from your previous social circles and you are left as the adjuster, those who were once your friends now question their own self-worth as if you produce less of a luster. Your significant other considers you to be their "project," they try altering your personality from crude to docile or from diplomatic to aggressive as your behavior they try to correct, the supervisor of your workplace terrorizes the shit out of the entire staff to drive them to be perfect, and it causes discomfort amongst your customers who may decide never to return due to such a show of disrespect.

These habits spread to the halls of Capitol Hill as political interns form mini-cabals with sealed lips, they selectively share information that can stonewall great legislation when the smallest thing slips, partisan opponents refuse to acknowledge each other's positions because they don't let go of their grips, and building an insurmountable wall of gridlock by everyone sticking to the dialogue on their partisan scripts. The party in power insists on controlling the entire debate, prompting those across the aisle to resort to extremes in an attempt to derail the inevitable tax rate, taxpayers suffer the most because they are subsidizing this juvenile mentality that is supposedly the most exceptional patriotic society to date, yet it feels an awful lot like a three-tiered class system candy-coated as nothing more than a slave-state.

Desensitized Death

In today's world sickness, disease, war, famine, drought, and daily horrors that the media feeds us only make us all desensitized, everywhere death is a daily occurrence and it doesn't even make feel emotion for those who had perished, some of us pray to give ourselves the sense that a Higher Power shall make it better, but the reality is only human effort, because that will only make us start to be more empathetic which will bring back a being who doesn't tune it out; someone more sensitized. If we all started donating, investing our own time, and joining humanitarian drive, these are the only things that will resurrect dead emotions, because this is what is needed of our actions to makes us once again bring back lost feelings; doing this will only make us thrive.

Our society has become so grim in our existence, when a neighbor's passing is as devoid of an emotional reaction, we are so emotionally flattened it's almost like we witness a spider devouring a smaller dead insect, we generally will put on a grim face for a moment and say, "You have our condolences," and that is the extent of our grieving action. When we hear of someone's death within the close circle of people with whom we communicate, we barely reach out to those who were close to the person, our biggest gesture is to send flowers, a card, a phone call, and even sometimes we are so pathetic as to merely send a text message, we share something in common with the person who just died, because we too are dead inside; it is no myth.

In our culture we are so desensitized to violence as it is in everything we do, we witness bloody deaths in our daily tasks, such as a video game we play for enjoyment that trains us early-on to have a warrior's mentality, this is desired by so many young men that they will even wait for the opportunity to do so in queue. Even when nationalism rallies us to prepare for war, it makes being a soldier seem like a valid life choice, even when our country is not directly threatened, because we have been brainwashed early-on to have bloodlust coursing though our veins to kill for fun; not even for a second does it look like a chore.

Video games can be fun entertainment or escapism that keeps life from being boring, always be mindful of how the characters in these elaborate simulations are merely props upon which you can exert excess energy, and training our young to admire warfare at such young ages; nothing but mentally flooring. With the sense of accomplishment they get when they go on a kill streak, the common individual does not realize how it warps one's mind, before they know it they are in a distant land with bullets hitting nearby walls; this is our youth who could be in bodybags before they ever hit their peak.

Serving in the military should be an undertaking for someone who wants to strengthen a sense of community, protectiveness, and create a brotherhood, for everyone who joins this military way of life, they will always quickly adapt to what is considered a comfortable daily lifestyle, the highest ranks running this show tells these young minds comforting lies, and that what they are truthfully doing is for the greater good. If you are enlisting in the military with a primary goal, you see a great deal of glory in thought of shooting up a bunch of powerless people, later in life you will never forget what you were commanded to do, and you will wish you could bury these haunting thoughts in a bottomless hole. The actions done in your juvenile mindset, everything commanded of you is an order of your country, and you may experience things that give you memories you cannot forget.

Lastly, let us not forget that organized religion has killed many more than the entire videogame generation, even with the advent of mechanized weaponry and bombs that get more advanced with each passing year, the strangest thing is this is the thing a majority of our economy is dumped into, and we still raise our flags proudly and anyone who is left with a peaceful mindset is somehow against our nation? Religion is intended to be an outlet for achieving inner peace, self-reflection, and doing good deeds for others, what about the coincidence that companies benefit from defense contracts, no one questions military revenue on any level, somehow when one of our own dies tragically in battle, there is a letter that can be typed up to let their families know they died as a "hero," and is this acceptable news to give to a grief-stricken, sorrowful, and bereaved mother?

Faith and war have a place on Earth, the most glaring abuse of faith or war is to use either concept in an attempt to intimidate or control others, and both systems that abuse their control over others are somehow supposed to fill us with mirth? From the very beginning we give our children action toys with guns, when they blossom into teenagers they all desire the next brainwashing of a first-person shooter, directly out of high school military recruiters are there to collect the ones who bought into this path, then they are shipped off to a war that is generally fought for protection or natural resources, the saddest thing is they think that the heat of combat is a chance to get in some kills, and the whole time they are excited because they think it is going to be nothing but fun. Desensitized death is what helps this entire process take place, they don't fear death themselves, and they have the mindset that they are off to better the human race.

Trying Times

In this fast-paced world that gets faster by the day, we live in a live that pushes us to our limits, it fills some of us with anxiety because the stress is always increasing, and some of us give up and end our lives because we cant take it anymore; we feel that is the solution, that is the only way. These aggressive lives we live in a corporate-dominated nation, it puts us into moments that can propel us to a point where it is possible to simply lose our temper, and it's all because we were not designed to fit in the existing machines that hold our minds hostage for a daily duration.

Our social ideals teach us how it is always best to stay cool, calm, and collected, some people preach the best thing for us to do is to maintain thoughts of an Eastern-based religion so we stay centered, that solution just makes most of us laugh internally, because long ago we became so dead inside that we just started having continuous thoughts of deviation. Once your peers witness you blowing up because someone triggers a nerve in your body that is a vessel of stress, your family, your friends, and your co-workers all label you as a "loose cannon," then people feel they have to watch what they say around you, they always walk on eggshells in fear of your emotions, because they assume if they say the wrong thing you will turn into a mess.

One should understand there are many reasons why people let their emotions override a long life of intelligent behavior, whether it be financial difficulties, romantic challenges, or a fear of failure, these are among the most common reasons why individuals allow stress to accumulate and eventually destroy them to the core, and then once they are so dead by being used and abused; no man can be their savior.

Then there is the problem of how others simply have a

misperception of how their friends, acquaintances, and colleagues view them, it blossoms from the desire that everyone wants personal relationships to run smoothly, and the last thing they want is someone to act, so such people can only do one thing; condemn. When any disruption to that idealized flow incites a toxic reaction from those who don't want to suddenly be thrown into the role of an outcast, this fear it affects every part of their thinking and every thought, and we know especially with social networks how one "wrong" emotional outburst will be permanently affixed to your past.

These fears can lead to a self-fulfilling prophecy at any time, once you fear you are being perceived negatively, a defense mechanism will inevitably kick in, then you will act out in such an unacceptable way that you will only create a tremendous uphill task of redeeming yourself, because of this you will spend most of your years feeling self-pity when you should just be feeling great by living in your prime. That might lead you to the behavior where you overcompensate by being too aggressive, too clingy, or too apologetic, these behaviors alone can also be damaging, because then people will view you as nothing more than someone who is pathetic.

What we should always keep in mind, whenever we see these traits manifesting in another, is how there could be something much deeper going on there, for example the person who is seemingly behaving like an oddball or a lunatic may simply be trying to fit in and gain a sense of normality, because remember something about all of us; we all came from a mother. If you identify strange or erratic behavior in another being, start by taking a moment to ask the person about your common goals and desires, as they could be quite similar in nature, you will establish a bond with someone who is obviously craving attention, and because you did this they might feel accepted rather than rejected; their worries will be soothed and they will not be fleeing.

This act is a critical starting point to avert crisis in any friendship, romance, or professional connection, when humans connect it makes the struggles they share seem less trying, you have a friend who is going through the same exact stress-inducing machine that is capitalism, and this will end the stressful times you both feel, and you both undergo something soothing to any mentality, mindset, or sect of theism; good old-fashioned human affection.

Gory Glory

The hate instilled in you corrects your vision as it gives the swiftness of your blade a cold precision. When the last gasp of air escapes from the lungs of a weaker man, because of your victory does not mean you get a longer life span. When you are nothing more than a glorified tactician your mission is to take others out of commission. Eviscerating the flesh of those qho pose a threat for a nation that pays you for the volume of your sweat. Silence those who dare to speak for the corporations that run the politics with a higher valued stock. The screams of the helpless are muffled by sounds of gunfire, and with every life taken you have to believe it is what is best for your homeland's empire.

The smoldering corpses with unrecognizable faces smoke in newly-conquered lands, and these nameless souls were slain by the most merciless of hands. Technological advancements in weaponry will ensure a bloodbath, which is nothing but a fast-paced game of eradication with a morbid aftermath. When nationalism runs in the blood of the societal majority, the ones who will feel the most pain will be those powerless in numbers because they are the minority. Dealing death has become a proud tradition, and with every new conflict that is created there are always those who are forced to fight against their own volition.

Nationalistic Napalm

There is a poison that stirs in a certain part of our population's blood and that is pride, it makes us monsters, it makes us demons, and it forces everyone without high-powered weaponry to listen to what we command, or their other option is to grab their loved ones only to run and hide. Weapons of mass destruction are just symptoms of this mentality and disease, the things that ignite the fervor of a nation is the suggestion that you can have pride in it, the reality is you can only have selfish pride, one admires things within oneself, and it sends others in distant lands who can't control the monster with weapons aimed at them only to their knees.

This only confuses these issues within who you are, that only confuses these issues into national pride, which then only produces powder kegs, and then we have a reason to assemble our military to go conquer places that are far. Inherently this puts nations in a position where they have competing worldviews, it is only driven by this pride, which only leads to conflict and war, and every time, no matter which side wins, people are killed and it's only human life that we lose.

All of this is driven by pride, which leads to conflict and war, admire your nation's achievements, also acknowledge it's failings that puts rationalizations in your mind which you allow pride to motivate you, and always this pride we find out though leaks in the media are because we were convinced to go fight, because people with the higher power lied. Admire your nation's achievements, also acknowledge its failings and allow yourself to ponder rationally about what motivates you, because there will always be those based off the actions of others that will experience some form of bereavement.

National pride just cherry-picks the best of a nation and rallies around that, it also personalizes this process in the form of an abuse of pride, which leads people to do things they would not otherwise do, and that in turn treats others who are less fortunate as nothing more than a war-torn doormat. This pride makes us think it is ok to win the fight with weapons that cause damage of unspeakable pain, as nations we need to have conversations about pride, what you can be proud about, versus what you may admire, as nations we need to decentralize, and most importantly we need to talk about what there is truly to gain. More power needs to rest

between you, I, and us; in our interpersonal relationships that we

can rightfully take pride in, this nationalistic napalm must end,

because that is a must.

Police Pollution

In a police state that is governed by a police nation, it does

not matter whether one is liberal, conservative, or in-between, the

society that populates the land is not far from any police station, and

our public servants use officers of the law to carry out their

marching orders while goose-stepping in formation. Be it to lock

someone up, to drain them of money, or to humiliate one in the

streets, the men in the blue uniform are the perennial threat dangled

by those in authority who give out financially draining receipts, and

they do it to get the plebiscite to do their bidding as they walk their

beats. If the people fear being arrested, they will behave

subserviently without being tested, and the politicians know this so

they put more police officers on the streets and it won't be protested.

The police flood low-income areas like the ghettos and slums,

and this creates racial strife amongst their residents that always becomes. Gangs form as a defense mechanism because of their occupation, drugs change hands to spawn wealth that was previously unattainable because of financial strangulation, and when status symbols and marketing rule, the masses' intelligence will be overridden by temptation. Then the police target the gangs and drug dealers to be the solution, they are thrown behind bars because of their distribution, and this leaves their families helpless and hopeless while they are in the institution.

The police force itself is never without its bad seeds, there are those who promise to look the other way when sinners buy them off, and because of power mixed with corruption they get away with these deeds. There are others who abuse their authority out of ego or lust, they expect their comrades to look the other way out of a sense of brotherhood and trust, and the ones with ethics have to pretend they did not see anything as they hide their disgust. They convince themselves they perform these misdeeds to provide the best for their spouses and families in need, they would lock up a criminal for the very same act but they still proceed, and they think that this way of life is one that will lead them to succeed.

Ignorant Industry

The majority of all corporate thinking is flawed and self-defeating, with a focus so narrowly honed in on chasing profits, when they should be chasing logical solutions that would truly benefit their revenue flow and functionality, and because of this mentality companies cannot stay afloat as their efforts are almost always fleeting. What these hegemonic entities fail to understand, is that by appealing to people's hearts and self-worth, they would be furthering their own stature in our global society, and most economic downturns they would be able to withstand.

More and more people are gradually viewing corporate interests through a critical and pessimistic lens, there must be greater emphasis on the common good, this will go a long way toward corporations halting this deterioration, they won't have to fire good people because of poor management, and will thrive in the face of losses that occur every quarter; their staff they would not have to systematically cleanse.

Holistic thinking is the answer at every level, with a richer multiplex of individuals becoming more aware of how their personal

actions can benefit the common good, then society would see them

in a positive light, and that would increase company-wide profits

that would make the executives only revel. Organic agriculture will

not only result in a healthier human being, it would also create

healthier minds and internal pride, they could be cultivating their

own forms of sustenance, and with a healthier regiment of nutrition

it would promote a general overall personal well-being.

Moving away from education models that are exclusively

standards-based, while incorporating qualitative forms of

intellectual evaluation, this will only lead students to infuse greater

self-worth into their studies of how the world works, and research

will be a priority that is done with haste. Gestalt psychological

reasoning will allow individuals to examine their own capacity, we

can better organize our erratic thinking into a logical thought

processes, ones that interact with those of our peers, and everyone

that is on the same page of thinking can work with tremendous

tenacity.

The current pyramid structures governing wealth and

power, they simply do not reflect human nature, they are built upon psychopaths overseeing a materialistic power base, and this will

cause the robotic masses to instinctively cower. As a species we

have many rich overlapping groups, ones that each of us can

potentially belong to, and to get into any position in life we have to

jump through a series of hoops. The roles a person carries out will

determine his or her unique interrelationship within the collective,

this happens to every other individual within the group structure,

these group bonds must be strengthened and diversified to revamp

the crumbling hierarchical system, and if they have no integrity they

will only be defective.

Hierarchy only creates resentment, anxiety, and fury, when

we should grow an interwoven multiplex of agents who govern one

another through social cues, and then objectives will be clearer

rather than blurry. Having complimenting vocal delivery with

appropriate facial expressions serves the purpose of reducing

ambiguity in reading others, and avoiding stress-filled sessions.

Soon will come the time when we can celebrate our unique personal

deviations, when normally we allow them to create divisions among

us, we can put an end to the ignorant industry that exists, and then

we can begin developing new creations.

Universally Unstable

Nothing in this universe is ever in a permanent state; everything

in this universe is always vulnerable, some things happen so fast,

and for other things all you can do is stare at your watch and wait.

What exists in one moment of time can be decimated in the very

next, the trick is to avoid caring what happens either way, and that

will prevent you from ever feeling vexed. This state of flux often

happens when humans are in a state of reckless behavior and

general thoughtless actions, we fail to conceive the impact of our

actions on others, because most of us do not truly even care, that

makes us lose touch with reality, and then we have no metal traction.

One with brilliant thoughts can have one's mental chemistry

become unstable; the complex brain will always be rapidly firing,

just because something is one thing now, does not always mean that

it will stay that way, and it may lose it's label. Machines inevitably all

need to be maintained, or they will eventually break down,

everything that is high will eventually fall low, because everything in

this universe needs some type of upkeep, or it simply will just not

sustain. Nothing is ever exempt from deterioration, everything eventually loses touch, and even the sniper's rifle in warfare needs constant recalibration.

Societies will crumble, nature unleashes chaotic states, which is its way of self-perseveration, cancers grow in once healthy bodies, and even the best Olympic sprinter may often lose his footing and stumble. Things will become infected and diseases will spread, in times of warfare one who is in the wrong place at the wrong time will die, because that random bullet from the machine gunner's nest will end a life with a small piece of lead. This planet is only a temporary teardrop on the face of an entire universe, its destruction is guaranteed, the only question is how quickly or slowly this fate will happen, when the end does come will we all be in a state of harmony, or rather, a state of a society that has turned completely perverse?

Our existence is irrelevant in that it's ultimately doomed, we may wipe ourselves out by our own actions, or the cosmos may do it for us, because either way you look at the end result of how this rock in space is just an isolated tomb. Either way, the evolutionary cycle will recharge itself, we will become nearly a distant memory to those who can try to record the uncanny events that happened here, because the sun will burn out in due time, and they will find evidence of what we did as they shave it from an ice shelf. Society is a fickle beast, people's values change in the blink of an eye, as do our personal tastes and capacities for judgment, there will always be more for us to take later, but for now, we need to start learning how to consume the least.

Our sacks of flesh-and-bone wither and dry out, our DNA gradually breaks down, when every time someone reaches the age when they hit the realization of this existential crisis, because just like the painting dictates; all we can do is stand there and shout. A shortness of breath can become a prolonged slumber, chainsaws work all day, so we have a newspaper to read every morning that will be resting at the foot of our doorstep, it's all because we have something that allows us to create oxygen to breathe, and at the same time, lumber.

In the end, nothing is going to be stable, if we accept how everything is meant to eventually fall apart, if we embrace this notion of inevitable decay, we can achieve temporary stability, and we can do it all without hitting a daily point of constant fear, terror, and lastly, dismay. This earth is universally unstable, stop believing everything is here forever, and wake up from your books that lead you to believe our species will always remain able, because that is not non-fiction; because you, my friend, are reading a children's fable.

Healing Happiness

When it rains the earth slowly tries to heal itself from this daily destruction we bring as we try to rise. The water makes flowers grow, which, when they blossom, makes the bright red cheeks of a lover show. Animals get water from pools that slowly fill; they drink what they can, and live another day without feeling ill. The roots of trees get sustenance, which causes branches to flourish and new leaves to bloom; which gives us oxygen so we can have breathing room.

The rivers fill, the crops grow, the rainbows appear; such a display of color makes us forget our internal fear. The soft tapping of the rain on the window makes two people hold each other while they watch what nature, for that brief moment, has to show. Some people actually go out in the rain; they let the cool drops wash over them, as they forget about the societal game.

After everything has fallen, and everything starts to peel, the clouds go away, the sun comes up, and we go outside and start to heal. This is the only process that the earth can do to repair the damage we inflict on a daily basis. We are killing our environment, and by proxy, ourselves; at this rate we will have no retirement. When things first started out on this earth we were just one solid land mass; and then, things started to change – and when they did, they changed fast. The tectonic plates started pushing us apart as the Earth began to evolve; and now, we are facing a climate change we cannot agree to solve.

You are wrong if you think this planet doesn't have a self-defense mechanism; more tornados, hurricanes, volcanic eruptions, and floods become eternally present. We are slowly causing our doom on a daily basis, as the ice caps melt and plastic builds up debris in our seas. If we ignore these signs and don't find something other than fossil fuels, we will have a broken machine to fix without a single tool.

The rain can't heal us from the road we are going down; the only thing that will help us is if we change the people's minds from town to town. There needs to be one thing that makes us finally stop abusing our only planet; because the rain will no longer soothe us,

and we will all just die on the hard granite.

"Men who become Gods can never fill such an ego in fleshy pods; forever at odds. "

"Energy passes through conscious entities in existence, and no matter how we try to harness it in human persistence; the path of least resistance needs assistance."

"Words of wisdom help all who can hear it, but sadly most prefer stupidity because it's easier to transmit; the reality is truth is scary, so in fear they don't commit."

FOUR

"IN ALL SPIRITUALITIES THAT RISE, WHETHER A PRIEST OF THE CLOTH OR A SHAMAN OF THE SKIES, BECAUSE THERE IS NO DENYING THE ENERGY IN OUR CRIES; THOSE DEVISE TO USE IT AS A DISGUISE TO THOSE WHOM IT SUPPLIES..."

"The mind's eye can be opened via chemicals engineered by man, because there are those on this planet who are waiting for you to join the clan; heighten your consciousness and widen your spiritual span – it always was the eternal game plan."

"Everything is infinite in time and space, and if you accept it you can advance to home base; progressing with the rest of us in the human race."

SPIRIT

Eternal Eyes

Human eyes only see what they want to believe, deep inside our
brains is the pineal gland with certain receptors that filter out what
we perceive, and when the right chemical opens them up there is a
universal consciousness we can receive. The mind's eye can harness
the true reality that exists on this earth, the Powers That Be don't
want us to tap in and harness this spiritual rebirth, but those who
dare to experience the information we hold back will be filled with
nothing but mirth. A substance harnessed by scientists who know
how it can be obtained, after it activates in your system the forces
that bond you will make you unchained, and in the flash of a moment
everything you could never understand will be explained.

Memories of your past intertwined with memories of your
future will be known, your consciousness will reach its apex and will
become full grown, and then you will join the rest of the population
who have entered into this zone. When you once thought everything
was divided, the information will flow through your mental core as
you will be guided, and then everyone will become one rather than
something that is multisided. You will weep at your past actions
when you acted for only personal gain, everything will suddenly
make sense as you now feel sane, and you will view the world with a

whole new compassionate brain.

You were blind as you ventured into a realm you can finally see, everything used to be locked but you found the one thing that gave you the key, and now you can choose every action that will lead you to peace; that I can guarantee. There is no going back to the way you once were, everything is a new experience and your past life only seems like a blur, because these are the reasons this small chemical exists and you will concur. After viewing this land with eternal eyes, you can only appreciate what exists on this planet that lives in the skies, and when your ego once made you a giant you are now shrunk down to your proper cognizant size.

Derailed Destiny

Everyone believes they have a purpose on this earth, there must be a reason we were the sperm that made it to the egg, there must be grounds for why we were born in this time period, because all of this can't just be chance; it's our destiny. We feel we are destined to do things in this one chance we get at life, some of us spend a majority of our lives chasing after one particular thing, something at one point in time guided us in a certain direction, and we feel if we follow that set path it will cause us less societal strife.

To believe that we are here for a purpose is rather egotistical, it causes more harm to our planet than any other philosophical notion, and what makes it worse is we combine the notion of destiny with something mystical. This is the way the Higher Power wanted things to be, it's fine that people are starving to death, children are being molested, and that to share news about our society that will be outdated in a single day has to be the death of a living tree. When awful events happen in our lives that are strictly due to pure chaos in motion, it ruins our entire week, month, and sometimes year, and we bitch about it to our lovers and cause quite a commotion.

It was my destiny to get that promotion, it was my destiny to get that new car, it was my destiny to win the lottery, and we let these things that we feel in our hearts that are supposed to happen to us put us in the worst kind of emotion. We are all blessed with a set path that was meant to be ours, we deserve everything that is supposed to be coming to us, we are those chosen people, and we are the ones who deserve to be the stars. Then when something doesn't go right with our plan that we pray will come true, there is always someone to blame why it didn't happen, it is always someone else's fault who got in the path; that was supposed to be yours because it was set in motion for you.

The people who believe in destiny are only handicapping themselves; they are only preventing their lives from reaching what their true potential could be, instead they are relying on one version of what they think should happen, that is why they only read one book, while the ones that could raise their intelligence remain covered in dust on the shelves. If what you think your true destiny in life is that suddenly becomes forever changed, it could very well be a blessing in disguise, when one thing doesn't happen, six new doors could open in an instant, if you think there is only one path to take in life; you are sadly deranged.

Life is filled with options at every angle each filled with endless potential, to believe that there is only one path to take in a world filled with open doors and possibilities; you are limiting your life to something some would consider a better option, which many would argue is much more essential. Mistakes are a wonderful chaotic blessing, they create new inventions, they create new cures for diseases, they create possibilities that were never meant to happen, was it destiny that made that scientist make the mistake, or rather something accidental that created a discovery that became extremely pressing.

Limiting one's mindset that a certain thing is supposed to happen for every person in existence, it's a belief that only holds back science in a terrible way, if we all believed we were destined to discover things, one would think that belief would surely kill brilliant thoughts and put an end to cognitive persistence. If it so happens that you feel you are destined to do something in your lifetime, if there are kinks in your plan, people hold you back, and things get in your way, cut through that notion that is holding you back, with faith in other things that could happen, you can pass a mountain if it is in your way; all you have to do is climb.

Empathetic Energy

The energy that radiates from the core of a being, it is an essence that cannot be seen by human eyes, it is only a force that can be detected by a heart that is in a receptive mode, once you feel it in another person it stops your state of pain, and once you finally feel that warmth is the time you can stop fleeing. People who possess a good aura will help you through any troubling time, you can tell by someone's energy if he or she is a good person inside, and it is those people with the inner radiance who will bring you from a state of crisis to a place that is sublime.

They have the positive energy inside them that others can feel; others know that they can trust this person when there comes a time in need, and it is this kind of being that will give you all you need, so in times of desperation you are not forced to steal. When someone emits this positive trait, they are the ones who will instinctively desire to help others, and the ones you know you should avoid, they show their cards early on when they lure you with their deceptive bait. The light surrounds the people of our world who lend a hand whenever they can, they have the true gift that the pure ones possess, they have the best trait a mortal can have which is empathy, with the ability to imagine themselves in the same dire situation, and that's why these are always the people you turn to when you have no escape plan.

This infusion of healing energy can extend beyond mere matters of a good attitude, it's this type of power that can make the sick turn healthy, the spoiled rotten finally turn a new leaf, as they show their first ounce of thanks for everything they are blessed with: humility and gratitude. When you have the power that can point you in the direction of those filled with sorrow, you can see the pain in their eyes without even asking them a single question, without worrying about what the current state of your rations look like, you are the very first one to offer if they need something, because despite how much you have to lend; you will always let them burrow. We always will gravitate to those with empathetic energy inside them, because leafs don't have anything to grow off of without the stem.

Delightful Darkness

We, as human beings, fear the unknown – which is the primary reason we are afraid of the dark. The world itself is rather dark, which is why we are afraid to try new things. We always hear horror stories of what happened in the dark to others, which makes us veer away from it and never think twice about going in ourselves.

People are always looking to get out of a dark situation, when they don't realize it is that very situation that makes the lighter times in life that much more bright.

No one wants a bad time, and we try our hardest to avoid

each negative situation. What gave darkness such a bad stigma in our lives? Don't the stars and moon come out when it gets dark? Aren't the streets less crowded during the night? Doesn't there seem to be more freedom in this time that everyone is afraid of? The truth is, just because you have less visibility in the night doesn't mean that you don't have something inside you preprogrammed to navigate you through it.

That goes the same for dark situations. When things get dark in our lives, our instincts kick in and we make the real decisions that mold us into whom we really are in periods of luminosity. Sure, there are predators who lurk in the night, but there are also more predators who lurk in the day – the difference is that, by day, they are just pretending to fit in to our society, which only makes them more dangerous.

In the day, you have to keep your guard up all the time; but at night, you can see a bad situation a mile away – and that is easy to avoid. How do you overcome this negative stigma you have towards the dark? Ignore that it ever existed. When the sun goes down, get dressed like you would in the morning – then venture without fear into the unknown. The unknown is exciting, thrilling, and most

importantly, you may find something that you never knew existed –
something that does not happen when the sun is up.

Perhaps even a "new you" is just waiting in that darkness.
It's idiotic to think, of all of the billions of people in this world, that
everyone of them goes to bed at night and works in the day. That
notion is just a statistical improbability. Don't fear the unknown;
rather, walk blindly into it, with meaning in every footstep – until
you find what fate brings you. Always remember, if you stand in the
dark long enough, you will eventually see the light.

Senseless Security

We, as human beings, fear the unknown. Just like the
Darwinian finches: long ago, we developed the evolutionary trait to
use tools to start building the society that we currently see. It all
started with the flint axe – a sharpened stone with a bone handle –
which was used for cutting. With each passing period of invention,
the tools we built became more and more complex – which only
evolved our tribes into something sustainable.

Soon we had enough tools that our tribes became bigger – so

big, in fact, that we had to expand within these lands. Some tribes

became so big that they started to divide and explore, which only

created new tribes who created new tools out of the new

environments that they developed in. We could survive and sustain

off these tools that we created, but then there was one thing that

these tools could not create, fix, or mold: fear of the unknown. What

were these forces that we were living under? What caused the

lighting, what caused the rain, what caused sickness, what caused

pain?

Because of the unknown, the concept of forces higher than

us were created. These forces were used to explain what was going

on around us. As we evolved even further, these were forces that

shamans would try and harness; but their Powers That Were became

useless. A song, prayer, or tribal ritual cannot control Mother

Nature. We were in fear of our crops dying, sickness spreading,

controlling the currents that run the seas; we were in so much fear

that we decided to mentally flee. We evolved even further, and then

Gods were created; so many, in fact, that that we prayed to every

situation that we wanted to have positive fruition.

Praying to these so-called Higher Powers seemed to work for

the masses: because if you believe something hard enough, it will come true – a self-fulfilling prophecy for me and you. Then, those societies crumbled, and along came the Jews. They created one God to pray to – combining tribalism with a strict system of beliefs to follow. They created rules to prevent people from getting sick, rules to make you spiritual, and rules to keep you humble.

The Jews had a flaw in their system: they created something so perfect, but not just anyone could follow with them. You had to be born of a woman with a Jewish womb to join this exclusive tribe. So what about the rest of humanity? They needed one God to save their minds and guide them through tough times. Then, one intelligent Jew rebelled – he spoke pure truth, and converted followers with his words. The Romans saw this as a danger to their existence as a people – so they crucified him, they made him a martyr...but that backfired and caused more anti-Semitism that would manifest and snowball later in the years...which, in turn, would end up being the Jews' worst nightmare.

Christians were born, and they spread quicker than wildfire. There was one God for every white man, and they had a powerful plan. Indoctrinate the masses with a book of teachings that would make everyone love – even though it lead to the deaths of anyone who wouldn't follow their path and vision. Then, another problem: Eastern people with darker pigments in their skin needed one God, too – so they came up with the prophet, Mohammed.

He would guide these people with one God – known by a different name – because different societies have different words for this powerful overlord. Then, we evolved even further – and out came the scientists. They had rational minds and very specific methods to prove things we feared, to show why things work the way they do. The Christians saw this movement as a danger – and then came the Dark Ages.

All science was destroyed, and we deevolved as human beings. We let fear become such a reality that it held us back. Finally, we evolved further, and scientists would no longer be held back. Then, science had a revolution in spirit – these rational minds would not be silent anymore, and everything on this planet has a science dedicated to it, and that's when we started to pick up where we left off.

Other religions started to sprout, still trying to control the masses with brainwashing – when all people have ever needed is love and a rational mind. Finally, we evolved into something that would save all of humanity – from that flint stone to the birth of the Internet: a universal consciousness to spread the truth. Then, the atheists could finally be free to express the true reality.

These people do not fear death, and are willing to march to their cause until we finally hit our final stage where we are all mentally evolved. The security blanket of God is there for a reason. "What will happen when my parents die? Who will I ask for guidance?"..."Who will watch over me, to make sure I do no wrong – I am a bad human being, and I need an overlord and a threat to send me to the worst place imaginable just so I make the right choices in life."

We are barbarians in spirit, and we once needed something to scare us into loving each other – but now, that time has passed. We will evolve even further, and the only real tool that we need – once we destroy all these people who want nothing but power and greed – is love...and love will come.

The time of fear is over. Don't fear the unknown: walk blindly into the dark, and be ready to see the light. We are evolving past the need to constantly fight. The security blanket is no longer needed – "Just be a good person," says the rational thinker, as he screamed it and pleaded...

Fanatical Flames

The time for integration of the souls that roam these lands must take place in this time, this is going to require work to change the way we think, we have a chance to change the way we look at one another, we need to diversify our social groups, we need to drop our egotistical reputation, because it is time for universal unity to create a land without stigmas; a place that is sublime. People must start to see in their day-to-day lives that people from many different cultures with all manners of colors and creeds, we must be encouraged to diversify and expand who we associate with and broaden our social groups, because to end this current system we need to start accepting every living man; accepting every type of breed.

This needs to happen so that a wider variation of views prevail in our established groups, the fanatic needs to lose his grip on the social mesh that he controls, radicals need to be stripped of their power, we need to breed by love and not by only our similar creed, because this alone will end the process that has always existed which will end this continuous loop. The radicals naturally form wide and varied relations, the more we encompass the fanatics in our social web, the more they become more radical in nature, the more they share their views within the culture at large, and this we have advancement and change in a more equal direction among us, because putting an end to these extremists of thought will create a better societal variation.

This will also serve the purpose of varying everyone's social milieu to a more heterogeneous understanding, a self-stroking cycle, essentially this can be remedied with a simple action which is making friends with a "loony"; let's end this age negative stigma, and let's stop labeling those who operate differently with this constant psychological branding. Let's fight this system that the Powers That Be try to enforce on masses: maintain, sustain, and most importantly, start by respecting the insane; educate yourself and learn that the mentally ill are not murderers who will cause harm, and do yourself a favor and take some mind-expanding classes.

If everyone just made an effort to include one mentally ill person in their social collection, the barriers would start to crumble and start to come down, by the same token by putting all of the psychologically different people together just reinforces stigma, and you will not have one single original thought among you, and your thoughts will be stagnated with never one notion of positive defection. Singling people out drives a fascist form of a fanatic; the ghettos will breed the exclusionary zealots, when in reality all we need is more communication between everyone, and those people who are sick won't feel as outcasts, because of your acceptance of who they are they will never act erratic.

Communication enhances, spreads, and broadens intelligent notions; start to diversify who you communicate with and you will remove the barriers, break this exclusionary system in place, when you see someone who can't help that they are being persecuted, let such intolerance light a fire inside you and release it, because when you stand up for those who can't help themselves you will create someone who will never forget what you did for them, and you will have someone who will always have your back in the times you need it, because with your noble actions you just created someone who will always under any circumstance show you unlimited devotion.

Forgetting Fears

We have reached the point in time where most of us can start to adaptively evolve out of this notion of constant impending doom, if we accept several universal truths about parts of this world we live in, we can end a majority of our daily suffering and self-imposed gloom. First, everything in life is just chaos in motion, from chemicals in our body, to our daily routines on Earth, everything is just chaotically bouncing around to reach its guided yet undermined destination, and we would live without stress if we just started to accept this notion.

Aside from the people who do evil in this world, mostly everyone in every population has good in their hearts, the media only tells us the bad things that happen, and because of this constant fear driven in our hearts our nerves unfurl. Cars will crash, airplanes will fall from the sky, someone who was healthy will have a heart attack, people will die of an incurable disease; we don't need to tremble in fear and ask, "why?" All of these things happen because chaos dictates the probability of random chance, we can stop pretending that bad things occur because of people doing actions that are no more than human nature; just be happy you are alive and continue to dance.

We don't need to let the fear of chance happening to us stop our daily actions, believing there is an omniscient punisher will stop us from living in happiness, and it will only make us turn on each other creating different factions.

Secondly, we need to accept that we will all eventually die, life is so wonderful at times the last thing we want to think about is the end, so don't let miniscule things that are unpreventable acts in society make a good day bad, because it will turn a life filled with truth into a being who will start to lie. Accept the Alpha and the Omega because nothing is eternal, live a life filled with laughter, joy, and happiness, and don't assume the things that you do will damn you to a place that is infernal.

Thirdly, everything we do in society is being watched around the clock, there are men who live in rooms watching everything we do around every inhabited block. Orwell wanted us to fear a Big Brother who watches over us day-to-day, what freedoms are taken away from us from this surveillance, if anything it prevents the men with evil in their hearts to act on their plots, and it prevents us from living in a safe environment in every way. It's not like these cameras prevent you from doing the drugs you like, getting a prostitute with a lawyer's salary, or binging on a lifestyle that makes you classless

trash, because of these cameras your head will end up on no pike.

They are there to document the crimes that do take place, so if you

have no guilty actions to hide from, walk right up to that camera, flip

it off and then let it see a grin of your face.

Lastly, everything we communicate to everyone in our social

networks is kept on record, if you act like an idiot and make a fool of

yourself, everyone knows it so accept how you are human and that

we all make stupid mistakes, and your remarks to the masses will

not have you die by the sword. If people scorn you for the things

that you say, these are not the ones you want to keep close to your

being, so throw the people with judgment in their hearts far away.

These four things alone, if you accept them in your heart, will help

you live with out fear, and you can live your life accepting that

anything can happen, you will eventually die, we are all being

watched in one way or another, so stop the notion that this life is

nightmare, and let your life truly start.

Soul Seekers

You are trapped in a lifestyle of choices that you don't want to make, and you want to be free. You look at the lock on the door in the room that you have been trapped in, but you don't have the key. There are individuals in this society who can open your eyes to the world around you, and these people can help you see. You wait in that room, until you hear the footsteps outside the door, and they have come for you, just as they came for me.

These are not the regular people you see walking around among the masses, for these people transcend all the classes. These people live in a world past space and time, and they are the ones who don't walk in the guided line. You can continue being yourself; you can be that dusty old book that sits on the shelf, or you can open your eyes and see what truths they have to extend, you can take the knowledge that they have to lend.

These people may have approached you in the past, but you were not ready then, your ears were deaf, and you could not see through the fog in the glass. These are not the people at your Sunday Mass, these are not the people who are ahead of your class, and these are not the people who will not let you pass. You need to break the mold that you were created in, you need to break the bondage of the thoughts of your kin, and finally, you need to break the silence, because it is no sin.

Let these people guide you into a person who has evolved, because you know your internal problem that you refuse to face, that eventually must be solved. Eventually, radical changes will happen and take place, and finally, you will wake up one day to look in the mirror at a whole new face. If you just took their words to heart, you paid attention to their thoughts and their time, one day you heed their advice and you will change on the flip of a dime.

For now, you still sit in that room, and you stare at that lock on the door, as you sit on the cold concrete floor. In time these individuals will present themselves, they will bestow knowledge upon you that will be your key. They will help your blind eyes finally see. I tell you, friend, keep your eyes and ears open, because they will come for you, just as they came for me.

"Comedy is an extremely effective psychological brainwashing tool that preys on the emotional response of the audience. A comedians is essentially nothing more than a drug dealer dishing out small doses of endorphins and serotonin per laugh."

"Music is a science. When you are making music you are conducting sonic experiments that you are determining will be aesthetically pleasing to the eardrums of the masses for no more than personal monetary compensation."

FIVE

THE ARTIST CAN ENDLESSLY VERBALIZE A CONTINUOUS FLOW OF NEW IDEAS THAT ARE THE NEXT OF THE GRANDIOSE VISIONS, YET THEY HAVE THE INABILITY TO GENERATE A PRODUCT BECAUSE THEY ARE LACKING IN MOTIVATIONS; TO BE DOOMED WITHOUT ANY OF THE EXECUTIVE DECISIONS

"Writing is no more than strategically and aesthetically manipulating a string of words to evoke associations in the human psyche that provokes an emotion for the purpose of communication, brainwashing, or trying to acquire monetary compensation for such an artistic form of expression."

"Everyone is quick to applaud; feedback indicates later that the idea was flawed."

ART

Artistic Anxiety

Minds that deviate from the norm need constant validation, they need the support of an endless flow of individuals, because if they don't receive acceptance for being unique that the rest; that fire that burns so brightly dies inside them and then there is no future creation. One can't really say negative things about the work they have toiled to create, they were only expressing themselves through a media that thought was acceptable, if they get a bad review they will emotionally lash out, because they want to be appreciated and if they don't feel the love they will only hate. The pain that they feel as they go through life with a mindset that they are unappreciated, it creates nothing but more grief for them as another deadline is placed on something that just happens organically in nature, and even if they create something that sparks a revolution in thought for merely one decade in time, and the tragedy exists that no matter how amazing their work is it will only become outdated.

Everything they do, regardless of its genre, before creating something they are filled with performance anxiety, they are as only as good as their last work and that mode of thinking cannot leave their minds, and if they create something that others do not adore; they only want to rip off their skin. They try to impress an audience or following they have attracted at any cost, their creations are how they put food on the table, and if they do not succeed they are just forlorn, hopeless, and lost. They need that human reaction that proves their existence had meaning, that the entire struggle was not for nothing, that it truly was worth it at the end, and at the end of the film the audience is clapping from the success of their first screening.

What would be the point of continuing to produce creative work if one has no passion for it, such passion is fueled by the hunger to entertain, rile up, amuse, and inspire the masses, this constant struggle is what makes success so mind-warping, because if they prove themselves they can have a big enough ego to act like a jerk. In capitalism the artist must be a businessman over a creative mind, they eventually have to sellout to what is popular to the desires of the three classes, and it's because of this system that brilliant work is extremely hard to find. In a Hollywood mindset everything is about quantity of revenue made, this warps artists into having to market to the masses, and this is what created a lack of intelligence in a product; this is what is killing the trade.

This inherent pressure causes artists constant grief and stress over what will be the next great "product" that glides down our own personal artistic assembly line, their voice is stifled because censorship is at an all-time high, they cannot let their true emotions be heard to society as a whole, and this is the reason why artists move to other countries that will appreciate their kind. These travails dance through the brain of an artist every moment of every day when the creative juices flow, they somehow still pull it together and create things to bring us joy in a colorless world, this is the artistic anxiety that comes with everything that is created, and these are the reasons why when you give someone your soul; you will have nothing left to show.

Blinding Broadcasts

Hyper hypnotic intentionally preconceived broadcasts endlessly blast, the machine that paid for by all of your combined sweat equity, and it makes you forget every lesson that your learned from all the moments that create the sum of your past. Defiantly designed to keep your intelligence at the lowest conscious level, as you never create anything new to express your emotions or desires, because it is easier to watch the lives of other people with more will and drive than it is to accomplish something that makes you internally revel.

When expression is a business first and a form of art second it kills your ability to think anything you can generate is worth revealing, any emotion you feel from the environment around you is bottled up in rage or dumped on socializing to people who just want to relieve a burden, and this is the process that has our culture stunted from growth; all the feeling of the expressionless glass ceiling.

Calculated Comedy

Emotions are contagious. Every time we emote something to another individual, we are transmitting our current mood to those with whom we communicate. Happiness makes other people happy. Sadness makes other people sad. If an individual can understand how to manipulate their own emotions, one can begin to heal other individuals. People tell jokes for two reasons. Firstly, when you can make someone laugh, that laughter makes the person who told the joke feel better about themselves, which, in turn, makes them happy. Most comedians are incredibly sad and tormented individuals.

Secondly, they tell jokes to boost the chemicals in their brains – so, for that moment when they are on-stage; they get high off the laughter of others. That's why so many comedians are bi-polar. They live their lives in depressive states; when they get on-stage, it is time for them to finally get high on life. As a former comedian, there is no greater high than when you can get an entire room to laugh. They feel, for once, accepted by people, and they relish every moment up there on that stage. Comedy is also an extremely effective way to brainwash people. If you go up on-stage telling the right jokes to elicit laughter, you are essentially nothing more than a drug dealer dishing out small doses of endorphins and serotonin.

The more people in the audience laugh, the more addicted they become to the person who is making them feel good. That's why if you have ever been to a crummy comedy club with people telling jokes that are not funny, you want to get up out of your seat and leave. The truth is that you came there to get high; when someone is pushing the wrong jokes on you, it has quite the opposite affect. The audience will question themselves and say, "Why am I still sitting here? It is time to go." Comedy is not an art – it is a science. You are scientifically arranging words to provoke the desired emotion, which, in this case, is laughter. Comedy is the most effective way to brainwash people.

Once you make someone laugh, they begin to form an emotional bond with an individual, because they are addicted to feeling good – mainly because we live in a world filled with so much sadness. That's why good comedians become so successful in life; they have figured out the proper way to transmit energy. If you make one person laugh in the room, continue on with your material – because with each laugh, you will provoke other people to laugh...until the entire room is filled with manic laughter. The best comedians are bipolar, because when they get up on-stage everyone is looking at them, which makes them happy. Once again, comedians are very lonely; when they have the whole room's attention, they will start to go manic.

Of all emotions, mania is by far the most transmittable with which to infect an audience. It boils down to energy transfer, which is why a good comedian who goes manic on-stage can get the entire place filled with energy and laughter – even if most of what he or she is saying is not necessarily funny. For something to be determined comical by our consciousness there needs to be at least one unexpected deviation present. This is why when you increase the number of deviations per selectively intentional comedic element it becomes increasingly funnier to the viewer, which then generally causes an increased probability of being spread by the current social dynamic of the comedic norm.

Melodic Music

Music intensifies every human emotion; the notes begin to penetrate your ears, and the algorithms enlighten you to a different notion. Music soothes the soul, inspires deeper thoughts, makes you feel happy, makes you feel sad; it can shift you into a good mood from something that was once bad. The sounds trigger feelings, and those emotions trigger associations; the auditory stimulation helps you through life's motions.

It can make you a rebel; it can make you a soldier; it can make you a lover; and it can make you a brother. It can inspire you to do amazing things – it is the soundtrack to your life, and it can cut through your ego like a hot knife. It can take you away to a beautiful place; it can change the expression on your face; it inspires you to finish the race.

It is a collection of carefully placed, aesthetic sound waves – and it keeps us going, it's a road that paves. It brings people together, it makes everyone feel the same belief; it has magic about it, and causes a massive wave of relief. It makes the insane man calm, and the sane man turn into a living time bomb. It unifies the masses – we are all hearing the same thing, and it does not divide us into classes. It is the new weapon of the future; people won't use guns or bombs, but rather, songs. Respect what every artist brings to the table – no matter the genre, no matter the label. It is the path to peace; we just need to take a moment to listen, and the violence will finally cease.

Artistic Aspirations

She doesn't let societal stigmas dictate her mode of thought, she understands the world we live in, and she's giving in so she can be bought. She will continue along her same path of artistic deviation, but strategically in a manner so she has capitalistic formation. Marketing will be the way she will manipulate the masses, when in reality she just wanted to take art classes. In America art is a business and a form of expression second, perhaps she will find a happy medium where she can be a force with which not to be reckoned. She is walking the line between what is a commodity sold to the masses, and what will get people jumping off their fat asses.

She lives in a city where art is highly valued, yet she will have to toss these dreams away to a corporation that chooses to pay. What will pull the highest yield for the pain and torment, an artist spends years trying to produce nothing more than a percent? She is selling out to the machine, because we all need to make a living, and she wants to be a mother who's incredibly giving. The people who surround her are rubbernecks who like a good show; the fantasies are squashed of hosting her very first art show. She lets out a soft breath of air, as she knows that nothing in this gallery can have any nudity, or even a female chest that is bare. She has a future to think about, because we all can't live this empty dream as an artist; she needs to rise above the crop and do what is financially smartest. Warhol is dead, and so are many other artists' revolutions, now she is left to deal with paintings and sculptures that are more or less just pollutions.

She has to be the anti-artist. The one who whores out the work for a set cost, as she crunches away on her calculator so not a single dime is lost. The death of the great American genius is long over in its time, now all that's left is the few who can barely produce work before it has to make the bottom line. Artistic aspirations were ruined by a clock; worried about what is next on the conveyer belt of inspiration.

CREATION

Creating Culture

The artistic brain is one that is constantly racing, with an obsession to create it is always pacing, and it always wants approval since validation it's chasing. Artists give society a different vision, they paint colors in a bleak world with the finest of precision, and they give clarity of thought to someone who cannot make a decision. They do not conform, allowing their consciousness to ricochet in every direction, they think about every detail in selection, and they do this all with the fear of rejection. They hope to inspire others to look past the frame, they try to be wild and never tame, and nothing is ever wrong; there is no shame.

The artistic body abused and expendable, there is no sleep schedule and every routine is bendable, and they destroy something mortal for something commendable. With an array of chemicals their mind is pushed to the limits of their sanity, they cannot be censored because to them nothing is profanity, and they do this all to better the culture of humanity. They never go through periods of sobriety, they always have silence their screaming anxiety, and this all because they must gain notoriety. Their mind fires in a way that is brilliant and unique, they are always mastering every form of technique, and they don't care if it costs them their physique.

These creations gradually chip away at the ceramic façade of society as a whole, they help people cognitively deviate because it is their goal, and everyone they affect changes their soul. They create followings of fans who seem like a cult, they create revolutions of thought for any adult, and they help lost people find their way as a result. They evoke every range of human emotion, they turn the silence into laughter by causing a commotion, they help the meek discover confidence just through a notion, and they do this their whole life all without a single promotion. The artist shares what they treasure about Planet Earth, they inspire others to do the same giving this planet mirth, and when you have the ability to express yourself it gives your soul worth.

One piece of art can vibrate across the masses, everyone can enjoy it no matter their classes, and they make people see more clearly just like a pair of glasses. They create music that everyone can appreciate, and emotions that people feel through song can never depreciate. People will spread what is popular by flapping their tongue, they will spread it though every land from the old to the young, and lives will be affected emotionally; it cannot be unsung. Artists create culture everyday, they do it for all genres and in every array, and when it is finished it goes on display.

Constantly Creative

The creative genius has an extremely rare psychological combination, they are generally obsessive because they cannot stop without frustration, they think everything must be flawless as they strive for perfection, and they work never ending hours just so they can get that next dose of validation for their creation. The innovator's art reflects his worthiness because he's enslaved by ego and vanity, he toils until everything is perfect, and it does not matter if he loses his sanity, and in the back of his mind he intends to better humanity.

These artists want not only to delve into the taboo and unconventional, they desire to touch the inner core of the viewer's soul which is more than intentional, and they will never use methods that are considered conventional. They all strive for art that will be considered nothing more than groundbreaking, these artists want to deviate and break the current societal norm with what they are making, and if they fail they will feel like a failure and their art has been forsaking. Every genre of which they think outside of the box can be the height of tedium, and they will do this everyday into the night with the hopes of creating a new kind of medium.

Many would accuse such a tortured soul of having no place in our society, without these chronic creators our lives would be dull and boring which would give us all anxiety, because of this pressure on their shoulders to change everyone's existence it is no wonder the artist never has a moment of sobriety. Artists rescue us from walking around all day as a mindless drone, we as a mass would only do what's in our comfort zone, and when we are stuck always expecting the same thing when someone does deviate our instincts would tell us to throw a stone. We want to believe we have a purpose for getting through a day of stagnation, we subconsciously yearn for some sort of deviated abomination, and that's why when we need something new and inventive we give it endless acclamation.

There are a variety of fates that may await the perpetual savant, if we do not cherish them when we have the opportunity a lack of doing so will only haunt, because these special people always give us something we want. The constantly creative may have to get lost in a drug-fueled haze, no matter how you feel about this morally you should only give them praise, because when you validate them their ingenuity will only blossom and their work will amaze.

Generic Genius

With the information freeway pumping intelligence to those who reach, there is a new mechanism creating a wiser nation that can endlessly teach, and the lands are no longer dying by those that preach; from this day onward the ignorant will wash up on the beach. They are raised by fathers who are corporate machines, they are kissed by mothers until they reach their teens, and they get anything that will help them grow by any means; they go to a yuppie college and smoke their greens. They deviate from the norm to make them stand out, they have big egos that are quick to shout, and they generally feel empty; in spite of peers who distribute clout. The run-of-the-mill devout boy scout on chemicals; about to sprout.

We've hit a time when people don't cherish the gifts they possess, these brilliant minds have no output due to daily stress, and we never know when they will shine bright; we just have to guess. A mind that only burns neurons when it is socially or politically convenient, and they brainstorm one invention as a contribution rather than six; grey matter that is lenient. Fear of failure should never hold them back, with all that wisdom they should be ready to attack, and this is why they are never given slack; with no performance one is a hack. Breaking the mold on a daily basis should not be a source of mental stasis. Fearing nothing should not make their output less, because everything they do should be a success.

They want to be recognized, they want to be the one who is prized, and they want citizens of the world to always find themselves surprised. Everything they do must be unique, they were born with a skill they must constantly tweak, and all this burning of the mind makes them weak; yet another modern Greek. They have a large vocabulary that they speak, they are constantly looking for a truth they seek, and generally they are called nothing more than a geek. Rebelling just for the sake of causing a scene, this is just a part of their daily routine, and when the virus hits they will create a vaccine.

They generally hate corporate slavery, they will launch their own small company with bravery, and no matter the results they will consider them savory. Everything in our culture must change, they will work in manners that are very strange, because they hope to the ones who will arrange. In society they are quick to boast an IQ score, the desire to be looked at as something that is more, and in the end they are nothing more than an intelligence whore. Generic geniuses are grown everyday, they do not work without a decent pay, and this breed of human is here to stay; the one who is forced to pave the way.

Writing Words

They flow on to the screen in algorithms of verbs, adjectives, and nouns, when they form sentences is when the associations make mental rounds, and if they are written properly; they break psychological grounds. The larger vocabularies grow amongst writers, the more passive minds they can turn into fighters, that's when these fires are ignited by the soul's lighters. One can rearrange preexisting concepts of the social norm, they can raise the awareness level of the consciousness in the reader all via an art form, and they can turn the future that was stagnating into a raging storm. Every word sends a ripple out there in time and space, they have the power to break the mold, and they can move someone to a whole new space; making evil men into good ones with a whole new face.

Writers are Gods who endlessly create, readers are the ones who populate the state, and when the two mingle they often procreate; their words keep even the sane up really late. After the consonants and vowels hit that page, whether it's a propagandist working for one's country to build a new age, whether they are an Avant-garde artist trying to make a decent wage; either way, they both create a societal rage. They are the screenwriters who pen a hit for the masses, they are a novelists whose writings change our states of classes, and they make the world see without glasses. Whether they are political, corporate, or just working for the general population, you can see them on your favorite television station, and you can read their work online with a cognitive stimulation.

Writing goes back to an earlier point in time, it spawns from the desire to keep records so humanity could stay in its prime, and it spreads a religious view that will make you feel sublime; also creating a new method of smoothing war crime. From clay tablets, books, and then the birth of the Internet-connected computer, whether you are trying to learn something from a tutor, or even just someone who is hacking to be an information looter; nothing more than a conceptual recruiter. Inspiring the philosopher, student, or teacher, one can hear others' words from your preacher, and when you want entertainment you check out the double feature; humanity is the apex of this language-based creature.

Things are written for political powers, the masses are controlled by church bell towers, and "benign" manifestos help to waste boring hours. They are written for personal validation, even if you merely recite one's quotation, and the affirmation of the alliteration creates the congregation; in translation, vocation, or simply a thought vacation. Whether it's done aesthetically in poetry to soothe the mind, whether it's a jagged word salad that makes you laugh in kind, because no matter the word combinations; if it's new it will always be a treasured find. Writing words is one of the hardest arts, whether it's done to top the charts, whether nationally-calculated political darts, and whether just there to capture our hearts; it is where humanity starts.

Word Warriors

In an age where the deadliest weapon is a large vocabulary and no empathy for others, it's the weapon wielded by politicians, propagandists, journalists, and single mothers, because it can make anyone turn on their fellow brothers. Whether it's a new act that is about to be turned into the law of the land, whether the only possible means to defeat it is a filibuster strategically planned, or whether it comes from the person with the most power who sends out their command. Sentences strung together determine the fate of an existing society, words so powerful they determine your piety, when spoken they only bring notoriety, and they effect everyone with ears; not just one, but rather, the variety.

A written language of these battle-ready visionaries tell the stories of our past, concepts of time flow onto the screen as characters are amassed, and just as quick as the brain fires; universes are created, grandiose and vast. The future as you know it gets created with each paragraph aesthetically built, with the precision of a watchmaker who feels no guilt, and with the care and compassion of a grandmother's quilt. Hours are lost and found at the same time, these thoughts evoke mindset that is sublime, it flows beautifully because the words always rhyme.

When characters form actions that represent the intention of divisional lands, wars can be declared when allies shake hands, and along with a cease-fire there's a list of demands. Blood will be spilled depending on languages with the most control, portions of conquered lands will not be distributed as a whole, and those who've perished will just be a statistical death poll. Then when the final mortars fall from sky, the same political lyrics bring peace as societies eagerly comply, and that's when the women and children no longer have to cry. Those words form treaties that transform ghettos into a developer's wonderland, warlords with death squads run massage parlors and day spas in their command, now that a slum has turned into a neighborhood master-planned.

Those who had originally sought out power to use the written language to distort the truth of the nation, those with promises that claim they will bring those who struggle to their well deserved salvation, and because of the naive who believe such men that only sell you temptation; their lies only bring momentary sedation. Whether the words are used as weapons to galvanize the rich, whether they are used for concepts that leave mass graves in a ditch, or whether truth is leaked to the people who will cause a revolution by an information snitch; make sure you're not just listening to a tyrant's snake-oil pitch. Word warriors create the dawn of a new unforeseen existence, saying the right thing only to write things with persistence, because they develop minds without resistance; always constructing humanity to go the distance.

Greater Grandiosity

There are three types of brains: ones that think within the lines of the boundaries presented to them in daily life, ones that think around the perimeters of the boundaries presented to them in daily life, and lastly, ones that dare to venture off into limitless areas of the mind. The ones that are thinking on the limitless side of things are often labeled as, "Space Cadets" – or people who think so far out there, they are too distant from the first two categories.

The Space Cadets are often the ones who redefine what reality is for the other two categories. When you are drifting off into the unknown, you will often find the true reality of the nature of things. It's those who dare to be grandiose in thought that makes others open up their minds to such possibilities. They will redefine where the people who think within the lines put their thoughts, where the people who think outside the perimeter place their thoughts, and they even inspire other Space Cadets to venture even farther out there into the unknown.

Often, these people will think of the new norm – the new standard – and they will raise the bar for everyone else's intelligence. Intelligence is nothing more than an old-fashioned arms race. If one person starts thinking one way, others will try to adopt that same thought pattern and deviate from it slightly to make it their own. Unfortunately, some people don't have the intellectual capacity to think for themselves – so they will just stick to what makes them comfortable: the lowest common denominator.

The exponential thinkers of our society are a lonely bunch; they are often viewed as madmen, whom others are quick to dismiss. It takes a fellow madman to understand a madman. The most positive quality of those who think on a grandiose level is often when a Space Cadet stumbles upon something he or she thinks is a new truth or standard; they will want to believe it so badly that they will often work hard enough to prove that it is, in fact, the truth, and that everyone had been looking at everything upside-down.

That grandiosity fuels their fire to success. When I was

working for a small internet studio in Las Vegas in my early-twenties, I wanted to create a show so badly; I just started putting random footage of me doing stuff on a timeline, trying to assemble it into a product that my superiors would like and "green-light" it. My first attempt was seen as "grandiose," but I still believed in what I was making. I took the original concept and forged a crude storyline into it, and then more eyes started to pay attention to it. I shot more footage and combined that with the first batch of garbage that had been deemed "unacceptable" to air – and, sure enough, it attracted more eyes. "Hey, I think you are onto something there."

I continued to build onto my vision, and, day-by-day, more and more people would talk about it. Then people started asking me if they could be a part of it. Then I got a supermodel involved as one of the characters in the show. That only attracted more people to it, and it only shifted people's visions into the realm of what I was projecting. After a week passed, I had the original people – who'd first shot down my initial project – requesting to be characters in the show themselves.

The project snowballed into something that no one thought could be possible – into something people started lining up to be a part of. Once the investors of the company got wind of it, they nearly

made it the flagship of their company – even to the point of secretly

offering me a higher pay than my co-workers – all because they

wanted to see my vision come into fruition for their benefit. Then,

the famous people started coming to the show.

 Then, the people who'd hated me at the office were suddenly

nice to me, and they would put up with an individual who was

looked at, in the beginning, as "too high-maintenance" – in short

order, they bended and set their schedules to whatever time

schedule I happened to be running on. The project became so big it

started to interfere with everyone else's work, and suddenly, my

time schedule was the new time schedule. After building what I'd

envisioned, other people would continually come to me with their

ideas on how they could make my show better.

 By the sixth episode, I completely lost all drive for my vision,

because I had changed everyone's perspective to my own – and I

completely improvised the entire show from that moment on.

Towards the end of the first season, certain visionaries – the ones

who follow along the outside of the perimeter – wanted to turn my

vision into their own. I was so burnt out by the project I had created, my mind went back into Space Cadet mode as I started to dream of my next vision. Someone who had taken on my thought process created the final episode.

This individual deviated my vision to fit his or her own unique vision. This was one of the people who had said the project was too "out there" or "grandiose" to begin with. It was just another example of a madman changing the way people think, making them conform to his vision once enough people approved of the radical notion. Seven years after writing, creating, and acting in my own series about myself, I was able to finally see the brilliance that everyone else could see once I'd adjusted their vision. I was too mad to even grasp what I was creating – and, sure enough, it was so brilliant that it was grandiose.

Serendipitous Sources

Where does it all come from? What made everything that is to be? Is it a pulse of sound waves, like the repetitive beating of a drum? They are the thoughts that created everything you see around you – from the most advanced technology, to the most simplistic devices, it holds society together like forceful bonding glue. Some people were born with the gift; others only admire those who have it – for it is everything that makes society consistently evolve and constantly shift. It is the ability for a human being to become and do anything, it is the inspiration behind the visionary, and it is the force that moves the swing.

Go to the busiest part of your city, close your eyes for thirty seconds, plug your ears for the same amount of time, and deprive yourself of your senses, and you will summon the source as it beckons. After those thirty seconds, open your eyes, unplug your ears, and take in everything that is around you; the source created everything you see and hear over these past thousands of years. From the cars, to the skyscrapers, to the electronics in people's hands, to the fashion you see people wearing, to the music you hear from a nearby band. The source created all of this, and it drives certain individuals everyday, to create endlessly, to make you want to inhabit your environment, to make you want to stay. The source makes a sane man into something wild; the source turns a grown man to act like a child. The source pulses through a certain percentage of the population's veins; and it is the source that keeps us progressing – it is the source that makes us sustain.

Others admire people who are tapped into it; they treat them like the stars of this life, when the source really just haunts these individuals who feel it, because it causes them daily strife. It's what makes writers write page after page, and it's what makes musicians play with such brilliance on the stage. This inner fire creates everything in this universe; it can be used for right or wrong, or can twist your desire into something perverse. It makes the words flow off of certain people's tongues; it controls people's actions, and it helps move air through their lungs.

Only those who found it when they were children could understand its true power; it is nothing and it is everything, and it can make the most monstrous of men instantly cower. It makes your fingers move across the keyboard as you type this sentence; it is not a preconceived notion, and those who carry the burden have no repentance. It can destroy you from the inside out; it can guide your thoughts to the proper path, or it can leave you in an asylum where all you can do is scream and shout.

You can see it in another person's eyes; the darkness that inhabits that gaze – it is a curse, but you view it as a prize. The source can give you the power to guide the herd; it can give you the power to control the land, and it does not give you perfect vision –

but rather, something that is distant and blurred. It is the power to

create something new that does not exist yet; people line up at your

door waiting to see the next product, but it is something that comes

when it desires, and you cannot control it – which, in turn, makes

you fret.

The source is the guiding light in a sea of darkness; it twists and

turns you, yet, somehow, in the end, you are able to grasp onto it,

and then you harness. It is the great chain that runs the earth; it

brings you nothing but sadness – but to others, it only brings mirth.

It is something you have come to accept; you can never get rid of it,

and it turns something rather dull into something extremely adept.

Be kind to those who harness the source; for they carry a great

burden with them at all times – and when they are gone, the essence

in their lifetimes that filled you with so much joy – after they are

gone, you will only feel emptiness and nothing but remorse.

Fountain's Flow

Close your eyes. Take a deep breath in, and slowly exhale.

The emotions will start to come like a flurry of hail. Dissociate. Tap into the source, let your words spill out onto the page, and they will have tremendous force. They are all just waiting for your action, because the world is a stage. Like a million eyes watching, just waiting for you to fill up the page. When you are forcing each sentence out of your brain, it is like forcing blood out of a corpse's vein.

When you let your emotions start to flow, they will have a tremendous amount of force, just like the winds in a tornado that blow. Just like a flowing stream that carries the falling leaves of autumn to a new destination, your language will prevent others' thoughts from stagnation. If you feel blocked in any way, perhaps that is just your soul telling you that you have nothing real to say. Go experience the world around you; let all things in motion inspire your psyche. Let life guide your thoughts and bleed your spirit onto the field in front of you, as if something pricked your person, like something spiky.

You have so much you want to say stored up inside you, the time is now, let this moment be your venue. Like the crack of a whip, like a coin that was flipped, like the water guides a ship, like a record that will never skip – flow! You have been trapped your whole life, and now, the time has finally come – you are ready to feel the

emotion when, your whole life, you have been numb.

Don't let the brick wall stop you anymore; break on through,

and levitate as your feet leave the floor. Close your eyes. Take a

deep breath in, and slowly exhale. Dissociate. Tap into the source,

let your words spill out onto the page, and they will have

tremendous force.

"Crazy is living in a world with crazy people who think they are sane; when in reality, accepting their insanity is the sanest thing they can do."

"It is your job to ride the mania, because the depression will surely ride you."

"Try not to think outside the box, but rather, think inside the circle."

"I am we, and you me, as I am you, for us to be a we: we must be you; I must be we."

SIX

NOTIONS OF THOSE WHO DESIRE TO END PSYCHOLOGICAL PROBLEMS IN ENDLESS DEVOTIONS, YET THE LABELS THAT ARE GIVEN RESULT IN OVERMEDICATED FLATTENED EMOTIONS; THE WEARY SOCIETAL COMMOTION.

"They said I could be anything I wanted to be, so I chose to be everything."

"All inspiration stems from validation."

"The death of the extrovert; the fear of silence from the introvert."

PSYCHOLOGY

Perception Preservation

Your perception can be dictated by your mood, it can be tuned like a fork, and it can dictate what you eat as food. A keen perception is all about looking at the finer details in life, you can be sharp as broken glass, and having a perception makes you see through the lies and deception, because it cuts through them like a hot knife. Thirty people could all watch the same crime being committed, everyone will have a different story of how things went down, because everyone perceives everything differently, and each perspective must be submitted.

Different drugs help people see things in a new light, some will expand your mind, and some will bring you so low you can't even fight. Your perception can be skewed, you can have blind spots in life, and it can make a nice man boil and brood. Hormones can fuel your perception, it can be fueled by emotions, and it can be biased based off your devotions. You can deny your addiction to happiness, you can deny the way it makes you feel depressed and sadness. Those with whom you surround yourself can also dictate your perception; proxy dulls your senses, and it can guide you in the opposite direction. Everything you experience is just a dream; your faux reality is no more plastic than a gust of steam. Having too much responsibility can skew your perception and having too little can degrade your intellect and give you poor reception. Money or material possessions can also warp your views, just sit and watch the television and look at what is broadcast on the news.

Start viewing the way you want to live, try to look at things from every angle, and start to take as much as you give. It's the way you look at other people, no one is equal, manners are lost, chivalry is dead, and all of this is caused by your perception which put a bullet in its head. Knowing all of this information can help you see the beauty life has to extend; it's all how you perceive things, no longer will the glass be half-empty or half-full, you will just see a glass filled with some water, and that's how you can change your life and put any misery you have to an end.

Dream Database

When we rest our heads on that pillow, pull our sheets over our bodies, and close our eyes for the night – what is it that we experience, exactly? Just like how different dreams can be interpreted differently to different individuals, I personally believe we have been interpreting what dreams are incorrectly. I believe dreams are chaotic firings of the brain, which makes us live quantum instances from segments that are parts of our daily lives stored in our subconscious.

They are a mix of every emotion: joy, grief, horror, and relief. They could be a sexual fantasy, or something rather abstract and fancy. Dreams should not be interpreted, because they are like trying to interpret the digits in Pi. Your brain is always on – it is always firing; when you dream, those thoughts are just there to entertain your brain with a faux reality while you attempt to get a proper amount of R.E.M.

Dreaming is like watching a movie. It's not real, and whoever wrote it is a Hollywood hack. It's pointless imagery to occupy your encephalon; when you wake up, you may remember certain parts and chunks, but don't use those memories of something that merely harbored your mental ship while you were docked for the night.

Emotional Entirety

We live in the land of emotional walls, we build them all our lives, and we build them a thousand feet tall. We are flooded by painful memories that make us avoid new things, and we let those old negative associations clip our wings. If you speed down one road you fall into a hole, and you will never go down that road again even if the experience may be different, because you want to achieve your modern-day goal. Memories can be painful, and you are no fool, you forget that sometimes the same road may produce a different outcome, which can sometimes be gainful.

We become distant from each other, we keep each other at arm's length, we choose our actions carefully, and we don't act like a brother. If we started practicing re-association, all the way down to our dendrites, we would turn into a whole new nation. Becoming emotionally available is a hard thing to do, when so many of us screw each other over, we just swallow a situation rather than just chew. We become fearful of one another, we have to keep our distance, and we won't let something blossom before we are filled with doubt and that hope is instantly smothered. Everyone is in complete separation, from the second we get in our cars, to the second we gather at that train station, our emotional walls are at maximum, and we keep everyone at a distance that's far.

The day we start to let down these walls, is the day that we become a society of understanding, and that will be the day we can openly accept everyone who walks down the halls. The past painful memories of those who have ruined times for the rest of humanity need to cease, and then we will accept there are more good people than bad ones, and that day is when we will regain our sanity. When we allow our emotional pain to rest, is the day we will start to be a society of true emotional freedom, and then humanity will no longer be a test. The day we start being emotionally available to one another is the final day when our emotional walls will finally be scalable.

Ecological Edge

We know the truth is out there; we get bits and fragments of it on a daily basis with those who make keen observations, but those who can really understand the reality of this universe; these people are rare. Some try psychedelics to expand their mind and the way they think, they go on a trip to another world for a few moments in time, but those thoughts they gain are only momentary, because they are gone when they come down; gone within a blink. Then there are those who constantly seek the knowledge of our true existence, they are truth seekers who wander this short time span we experience called life, they find a substance that gives them the knowledge of the universe and then they start on the path of resistance.

After they drop it on their tongues the lysergic acid diethylamide takes effect, all of their blind spots that their brain has been keeping in the true reality of this universe are suddenly revealed, they see the universe for what it truly is, and from that moment on they want to start to defect. You simply can't go back to the life you were living, after those photoreceptors in your pineal gland are blocked, all the lies that your brain has been telling you, you break down and this life you have taken so much from makes you want to start giving. The knowledge of the universe is now solidified in your brain, you can never look back at the old life you were living, and you suddenly want to break free from your egotistical bondage that holds you together like an iron chain.

You have hit the peak of everything you could possibly know; all from ingesting a fungus that grows on rye, you are mentally changed forever, and now with this knowledge you can choose to change the world for the better, or you can torment yourself by knowing the reality of this universe while still putting on a show. The substance is highly illegal for a reason, if everyone tapped into this source of immense power we would all deviate from the norm and such an act would be considered nothing more than treason. As children we are brainwashed that drugs are bad, how they could cause brain damage, make you a criminal, turn you into a deadbeat, or become someone that is nothing but mad.

I learned how a little bit of brain damage could be a wonderful thing; sure, you are fried for a few months after acclimating to a world of pure truth – but then you heal, become sane again, and from there it is nothing but an upward swing. People will tell you, just from the thoughts they hear come out of your mouth that every word you speak is nothing but something that is more than true. I could list off the great minds who dared to venture into such a realm; their enlightened thoughts changed the world we see around us, so much so that it would overwhelm.

The brave try something that could damage them forever, they could turn into a space cadet who is so distant from normal human thought, or they could overcome and let their intelligence guide us into a world filled with the definition of clever. I was insane enough to travel into the world of the unknown, and what I found was a beam of light that contained nothing but pure knowledge, and from that day I was forever changed, because I had entered the zone. I dared to walk to the edge, I ventured into a state of complete human understanding, and here I stand now, and I did not fall off the ledge.

Tremendous Trauma

It happens in a flash of an instant – it's the sum of all your fears; you feel the terror in your gut, and you are in a situation that that only brings tears. You can't believe this is your current reality; you wish you were anywhere else, but you are forced to deal with factuality. You are past the point of dissociation; your limbs go numb, and this is the moment in time that will haunt every association.

Panic spreads throughout your person; you close your eyes and try to think of anything else, and your hyperventilation only makes your symptoms worsen. Anxiety floods your emotionless shell; you are paralyzed – and at this very moment, you are in the deepest bowels of hell. Once the moment is over, it will haunt you for a lifetime; you may never get past that minute of anguish – and because of this, who you once were slowly begins to vanish.

It obsesses in your dreams, and that single stored memory makes you wake up in screams. It is a part of you now, something you will carry for the rest of your life; something you will always have to face, causing you a great deal of emotional strife. There was nothing you could do to prevent it; you blame everyone else, you won't accept that's the way life happens – not one bit. It affects you on a day-to-day basis, and it affects your thinking; it affects your emotions, you are wounded and you won't stop bleeding.

You turn to anything that will give you relief – no matter how much you cry it out, this life robbed you of something, and you only hate the thief. You turn to professionals, you turn to people on the street – you turn to anyone you fucking meet. Cure me of this pain, erase this memory, you are a haunted soul, for the love of God – cure me of this grief.

No drug can soothe you, no doctor can fix you, and no Scripture will enlighten you – for you are caught in despair of a memory that won't repair. Everyone around you can see how much pain you are in, and they are concerned – but they don't know what to say to a soul who has been burned. Then you hit the moment of your salvation – you realize there is a way to fix this through re-association.

Replace that horror by thinking of something that gives you joy; slowly with time, consciously doing this act will make you no longer be that trapped, scared little boy. Soon you will repair the way you think; that trauma you once experienced will be gone by the time you blink. Your mind has the ability to fix any wound – you just have to be conscious enough and newly-attuned.

That what once scarred you for a majority of life – all those repeated memories of the inciting incident, and you will cut through with a mind so sharp it is like a knife. You will become stronger, day by passing day – and then, the most beautiful thing will happen: you will forget what took the color out of your life, which only made you see gray. You will arise everyday as a stronger person, because you beat the trauma; now you know in your heart that nothing can put you in that place again, and you will live your life free from drama.

Debilitating Demons

Whether we were born with that thing that will eventually come, we developed them through grade school, even if they came later in life during college, even when we started our career, inside all of us is that one demon we cannot battle alone; the demon in which all of our problems seem to stem from. Some of us use drugs to self-medicate, others try to exhaust the demon inside them with exercise, some get angry and destroy physical property, and the ones with a peaceful soul can only sit there for hours on end as they quietly meditate.

The demon comes out in you when something hits the trigger, others may try to use cognitive behavioral therapy to calm you down, but if they don't know what they are psychologically doing they will only make that demon two times bigger. Sometimes you will snap at a loved one for no reason at all, sometimes you will get blackout drunk because you want to forget it exists, and sometimes that demon leads you to the edge, and then unfortunately down you will fall.

We all have one of these monsters that reside inside of our core, it is foolish to pretend we don't, if we all just recognized we are all in some type of pain perhaps we could start to heal each other, then there would be less suffering, and out of life we could all get so much more. We don't need to abuse the ones we love, we don't need to neglect our offspring, we don't need to treat our coworkers like trash, because we can all be the person who opens the cage and releases the dove.

Violence can be non-existent, murders will no longer be a societal issue, there can be fewer police on our streets, and we can start to care about our fellow man on a basis that is persistent. The way we kill these demons inside us is a very simple solution, it's something we all have forgotten how to do, we all need to do so to end this inner torment in a very simplistic manner, and the way to do is by beginning to talk to one another about what is bothering us, rather than turning on the television and taking in nothing but mental pollution.

We forgot how to communicate as a society, because of this we let the demons inside us fester, we bottle up what bothers us, and then we go on a killing spree seen many times in the past, as it has become a garden variety. When you vent your problems to another soul, chances are they might be going through the same thing, we are all just human beings living similar paths of life, and statistically there are a majority of us stuck in the same hole. We don't need therapists, psychiatrists, or pills from pharmaceutical corporations, we need to stop fearing that people are going to judge us on what we are going through as a person, we need to accept one another's problems, this notion alone can start the slow process of reconnecting with ourselves as people, and then we can rebuild nations.

We should feel no shame in the monsters and demons residing inside of our being, there are seven billion people on this earth, a large number of them are going through the same thing you are, stop pretending as though what you are facing in life is condemnable to death, start communicating to your friends about what you go through instead of putting on a mask, pretending you are happy all the time, and for once in your life stop avoiding the situation you constantly are fleeing.

I tell everyone I meet what my psychological and mental problems are, it disarms them completely because no one is ever truly honest about their situation, then they disclose what ailments they possess, we share an intimate human moment of mutual understanding, it brings us closer as members of society rather than what you would think would happen, which is to make them distance themselves and keep you far. Talk to people with a good aura around them, share your stories, share your ailments, share your demons, and then be shocked as a human connection is formed, and a friendship between two strangers begins to stem.

Emotionally Eviscerated

People with a low intellect physically fight; they don't know how to express their rage, their education is juvenile, and all they do is work out at the gym, and are ready, at any moment, to battle. Then there is the complete opposite side of that mentality: the intellectuals, who have a much deeper psychological brutality. It takes five sentences out of a human being's mouth to properly psychoanalyze them: you look at the clothes they wear, and how they style their hair – watching their micro expressions, analyzing their body language to identify their true intentions.

Then your tongue can begin to spray toxic sound waves straight into their brains. Strings of words so damaging to the psyche, they will try to drown it out; your words speak softly as you weaken their entire existence, and they can only do one thing: start to shout. Their moronic insults only fill you with joy – and you manipulate them with more words, like a child plays with a toy. It takes only a few short sentences of pure truth to render them disabled, and you have dominated them with a brain that is enabled.

Don't be fooled by someone's size, because you can see the power that exists inside him or her by looking directly into his or her eyes. The brain is more powerful than any muscle, and if they do choose to strike you for the damage you have caused in their ego – just call the police, since they struck first, and straight to jail they go. You could file a lawsuit with your lawyer, you could file a restraining order; but instead, just let the words you said seep into their subconscious, and you will be their destroyer. Just because you have muscles does not mean you are in control; it is the person who has read the most books who will make you pay the toll.

Watch out whom you push around in society – because, one unfortunate day, you may meet someone who will leave you emotionally eviscerated...those words will haunt you for an eternity, and, instead of violence, you, my friend, should have waited.

Alert Attentions

With a mind that moves at a faster pace than the others in society, you have poor grades because you can't focus at the slower paces of the typical variety, and then you are labeled by a pharmaceutical pill-pusher; it creates internal anxiety. They say the way your brain works is considered a disorder and you require medication, they choose to alter your brain with stimulants to give it formation, your mental chemistry gets altered to enhance your focus duration, and you are forced to work harder for the betterment of the work flow in our nation. The chemicals push your cognitive abilities into overdrive, the rest of your life you will be medicated just to stay alive, and it's all for the betterment of the status quo; just to make you strive.

Every day you take that pill to make you concentrate like the rest, for thousands of years we lived without these substances but now we have progressed, and now you have to push yourself to the maximum just so you can be at your best. You become obsessed with your own daily workflow, you try to make each day more productive than the last just so you fit in with the show, and eventually you have to keep increasing your dosage because of your constant plateau. You must meet the expectations of the people in your pack, you must be on a continuous overdrive so you stay on track, and it's all because of the man who writes the prescriptions; the person you pay to be your quack.

After a few years of this you forget what it was like to think at your normal pace, you are just a chemically-altered rat who is running the race, you apologize anytime your mind drifts off into outer space, and it's all because of the money we are all forced to chase. The pill just becomes a part of your routine, your alertness must be top-notch because you always must be keen, and the people who have this disorder pay for a cure just so their wallet is always green. In this Land of Opportunity you have alert attention, you must retain everything with adept comprehension, and there is no place for those born with genetics who defy what the masses deem as convention.

Lethargically Lost

Let your moans of agony echo through the caverns of space and time; you are just lost in the feed. Everyone looks at you like you have the biggest need; you are only viewed as an individual who lusts for greed; they see your words, but few care to even read. You have been muted, you can shout as loud as you want, because you are mentally booted. Take your label and let it define you in everyway, there is no soft landing for you, my friend, so it's best if you just walked away.

You are just the baby who continues to cry; it has gotten to the point where no one even asks, "Why?" Just let it writhe in pain, there is nothing you can do to soothe it, and there is nothing that it can gain. You become nothing more than words jumbled together on a screen, some hope you come clean, but you have become nothing more than a machine that needs to ween. They should have never taught you how to talk, you run your mouth all day, and by the end you can't even walk. You have become the parrot that constantly squawks, every word you say is nothing more than the yammering sound of a talk box.

What an oddity to try to understand, just copy-and-paste what it said, because anything you say will just go to its head; all it needs now is a dose of nine-millimeter lead. Don't let it know you are on to it, don't give it what it wants – not even if it throws a fit. Like an infant sucking on a tit, all it wants is more, when in reality it is so dead inside it doesn't even give a shit. Stand back and watch it destroy itself, let the dust collect on it, and leave it on the shelf. There is no need for an intervention, only praise it when it does good, other than that – it's not even worth a mention.

I think I have seen just about enough, a tongue constantly flapping nothing but egotistical stuff, and its thoughts just seem to come right off the cuff. It's just skin and bone, it will bury itself in debt with another loan, and there is nothing you can do to guide this immovable stone. Give it another empty gesture, because soon it's a cow that needs to go out to pasture. You will never get to know the real master, so do your best to avoid it, because you can't get away from it any faster. The one with the biggest need is always just lost in the feed.

Analytically Alone

You were born with an abnormally high perception for the operation; you notice the little things about everything, which only helps you understand how the bigger things function in every social medium, mechanical machine, and corporate workforce; when you know how the system works it leaves room for your own personal deviation. You know the quickest way to get what you want, you know how to cheat the system devised for the masses, and when a figure of authority catches you in the act of breaking the rules, you excel at playing the idiot who did not know any better and no one can smell your front.

You beat the traffic on the roads, you avoid the lines in the places you shop, and you just know what to say when it comes to a group effort, all so you don't have to be the beast of burden who carries the heaviest load. You see flaws in the systems created for the masses; you go directly to the leader of every group to suggest changes for the betterment of our societal organization, and because of your perception, despite the money in your wallet you can transcend through any of the three classes. You perfect things that haven't even broken yet, your intelligence is always recognized above the rest of your corporate comrades, and when a problem arises you get excited because it's something new for you to figure out how to fix, rather than what other people do which is worry and fret.

Because of your ability to see how everything in this society flows, you are placed in a breed of people of whom there are only a few, with your intelligence you don't fit in with the rest, and because you notice every little thing, your group of friends never grows.

Intellectual isolation is something you should get used to quite fast, no one likes the genius who understands everything, and having a life of solitude is something you better be prepared to last. Like a human microscope that can magnify every situation to a microscopic level, your emotions get flattened, and not even a discovery of your own doing that causes praise from your peers elevates your mood enough to make you revel.

Your mind is always running, evaluating, comparing, and you will have daily revelations of thought from your extreme moments of clarity, then the point comes when people expect such brilliance to come from your mouth, it makes you not even want to speak, which makes you lose your humanity; when you say something normal it is a rarity. You have lost your touch with the rest of your fellow man, your thoughts have isolated you from the rest, your own brilliance has desensitized you to what you even think is intelligent, and your loneliness only makes you do things that shorten your lifespan.

You wish you'd never started asking questions on why things operate, you become bitter inside from solitude, then those who envy your thoughts have to let you go from the flock, because you have become so distant you will not cooperate. Society sickens you in every form, you can't understand what drives people to do repetitive tasks day-in and day-out with the result at the end of the day, you deviated so far from the people you once knew you have lost all feeling of what it is to fit into the norm. You become a shut-in, you never leave your house, you are too smart for your own good, and now what you know depletes any and all drive and you will never win. Your analytical mind caused you to be alone, it was a gift and a curse, now you are left with no one to call, and all you can hear is the sound of a dial tone.

Imagining Image

From the second you look at yourself in the mirror in the morning, your ego tells you what you want to see, then starts the parade of delusion, you start to shape yourself into the image you want to see in your reflection, and you do this everyday without any warning. You put on your underwear that is your favorite style; you put on your clothes from your trendy designer, you start to build your character off of such trivial things that make you feel like you have an identity, and when your costume that you devised makes you look in that mirror and you give yourself a smile. You put on cologne or perfume that you feel makes other attracted to your manufactured scent, you do your hair the way you like it, you put on your daily disguise, and you leave your domicile that you feel you deserve even though you are overpaying rent.

You go to your job; you reflect a personality you feel other people psychologically accept, you know who to be nice to and to whom you can act like a total snob. You work all day putting on a façade, you do the bare minimum of what is expected of you, and when it comes time to clock out, you can end that portion of your daily façade. You go to your car that you strategically picked out, it represents you on the road, if you have a nice car people admire you, and if you have a clunker when someone cuts you off you don't dare to honk or shout.

You go shopping to buy yourself more items that you feel reflect who you are as a person; you have to have the latest cell phone, you have to have the latest computer, you have to have the latest designer clothing, and all of this imagery makes you lose who you really are; you only become a consumer whore and every day it will worsen. You eat at the restaurants that you feel reflect who you are as a living body, when you don't get a table right away, you get pissed off, you are not just one of the masses, because you are something fantastic; when in reality you are just a glorified ego who is no more than gaudy.

You are just another image with no internal core, you are a dressed-up husk of a being that is nothing more than a materialistic whore. You are brainwashed by material possessions, magazines that tell you who to be, television advertisements that make you want a product, you are nothing but a idiot who fits in with the masses, you think you are unique by the items you buy, but you will never be anyone because you haven't learned any of life's lessons. Just a mindless drone motivated by a lack of intellect to see who you really are, you don't read books, you don't educate yourself, and in your deluded mind you think you are going to the moon, there are no limits to your potential, because in that mirror you see someone who is only going to go far.

You are the puddle of water collected on the street after it rains, you are shallow, mindless, and driven by an image you feel is the "real you" when you are nothing more than vain. There is nothing at the core of your being, you have no inner spirit, you have no soul, and if you knew the true reality of yourself you could not take it and it would send you fleeing. Next time you look in the mirror look past what your ego wants you to see and analyze your image, change your habits that make you no more than a tool, fight to know who you really are, take control and then start to scrimmage.

Ego's Echo

It's the reflection we see in the mirror. It's the car we buy. It's what makes us cry. It's the clothes we wear. It's what makes us feel rare. It's the house we live in. It's what leads us to the places we have been. It's the people we associate with. It's what makes us believe the myth. It's the children we create. It's the skin color we hate. It's the things we say. It's what drives us all day.

It's the way we represent one's self. It's the unread books on the shelf. We can't seem to live without it. It's like a drug we cannot quit. It's what makes you look the other way. It dictates the prayers we say. It's what makes us judge what others do. It's what chooses which potential mates we screw. We can't live without it. It's why we always look for a perfect fit. It makes us seek validation. It's our constant inner narration. Every day you try and make it bigger.

It's why we obey the commands of others and why we pull the trigger. As a collective it makes us do atrocities. It's what makes us travel at different velocities. It's what turns human beings into dictators. It's what turns us into traitors. It's the one thing we can't seem to live without. It causes all of our doubt. It's our ego. If you can't learn to drop it, you will always just be a one-man show.

Vicious Validation

We all seek it; it was engrained into our beings at an early age, when we first started going to school, if you had good behavior and you did what you were told, you got a sticker, and that's what started this need to be accepted, and it only created a mental pit. Then later it became about grades, you had to complete your homework and do well on tests, so you could bring those good marks to your parents so they could throw you a validation parade. Some parents used motivational tools like bribes to get you to behave, while others would do nothing but scorn you if you didn't pull the good grade.

In college it became about your career, you needed to perform well so you would pass the class and when you worked hard enough to meet the demands of your peers, you would look at your grades, and if you met your own expectations you would release an internal cheer. Then you win a career in the field that you designed, and you work day and night to perform for your superiors so you would be validated by praise and a pat on the shoulder, hoping you would get a promotion or a raise with feelings that you felt you deserved, as so you were inclined. Then came along the social media medium, a place for you to express yourself freely, to post how you really feel about the world you live in, a place for true freedom. You are forced to silence who you really are; what you really think at work, to your lover, and even to family members such as your fellow brother, there is an finally an outlet for you to venture your opinion in a land that is vast and far.

You think you are free, but you are still a slave, because every time you log on you look for that little red notification to see who really cares if you exist, and you strive for that validation so much that you mentally plea. I hope what I posted makes other people happy, I hope my thoughts impact the world, I have to exist in this world that I strive so hard to make it in, and instead when you read those notifications they are just empty thoughtless comments that are no more than sappy.

We have become slaves to that little red box that tells us which other people approve of our existence, we even scour the internet to find clever, funny, and beautiful things to make others care with diligent persistence. The scientific term for what that little box that makes you log back on every time is called a reward band, when that time comes and you see that no one has even responded to what you have posted, you feel empty, you feel inadequate, and you feel like you don't even exist, you no longer are the flavor of the month, because you have become stale to the masses, nothing more than bland.

We will continue to log on everyday, post things that make people want to care that you exist, we are nothing more than beings who want to be accepted, and that notion alone makes us stay. I am no longer a slave to that notification box, when I log on, I don't care about the number it displays, I have outsmarted the system that keeps me coming back like a wise fox. When you log on don't get joy out of what that small window displays, beat the mentality, stop being a slave and don't even lend a gaze. If you continue to be manipulated by the validation station, you will only be part of the rest of the nation.

Barely Better

For some of us there is no better, there is nothing that medical science can do for us at this point, you can take the pills, you can see the doctors, you can write your suicide letter. I know you will get well, I have been praying, we are getting you the best medical treatment, maybe if you believed in God you wouldn't be in this hell. You have been to the institutions, you have been to the therapists, and you have been to the counselors; for you, my friend, there is no solution.

You are a psychological obstacle course, every doctor you see diagnoses you with something else, and you are a new breed of mad man you are an unidentifiable force. You can manipulate any psychological test; you have taken so many of them, that you know how to fool a trained professional, because you are not like the rest. In society you are a ghost, when people confront you in society, you just mirror their personality and people always like what they see in you because you are just a reflection of the being in front of you, and their narcissism kicks in so they like you the most.

You can't change what you are, there is no pill to take for it, you have an adapted social trait, and it magnetizes everyone around you; they come close when they should go far. You have memorized every possible human conversation, so how could you not bend people to your will, how could you not use your gift in small doses of manipulation? Your consciousness is split in two, when people talk to you they are always wondering which person they are communicating with, and which one is the real you. "It will get better," your loved ones say, they are blinded by the reality of your nature, and the only thing they can do is pray. You are an outcast if there ever was one, yet your chameleon-like nature makes everyone like you, they yearn for the light you provide, just as the earth needs the sun.

There is no better, there is only worse, when people try and better you they only destroy you even more, which is completely perverse. You just want to be left alone in a confined room, you loathe society and the way you turn into everyone you meet, and everything about this life will only cause you gloom. When you expose yourself to the medical professionals they look at you like some type of specimen who needs to be known, you were born into the life of a lab rat, and you cannot develop in this environment, you will be forever stunted, and never will you be fully grown.

I have learned when someone tells you they will help you get better that those are deceptive lies, they only want you as a specimen, and they just want to put you in a box and do nothing but analyze. I have been called an anomaly, a gift to humanity, a blessing in disguise, and these are all phrases that are no more than a homily. I will never take another psychological test, I will give no more of my blood, no more scans of my brain, because I have finally reached the point where I just want to lay in my bed and wait for the eternal rest. In our society better means worse, we are still in the dark ages of medicine, and the medical community needs more funding to advance itself, which they will take directly from your purse.

Passive Punishment

Ever have one of those friends who feels the need to punish you for the way you used to be? They want to keep you pinned down to that label you were at one point in time because they themselves struggle with a similar problem. They feel because they never acted out like the way you did that they can hold themselves to a higher standard than, "What you are."

In the past you found out that you know where they come from – the same space, time, and mindset you both were created in, yet sadly because of their seething hatred that they will only watch silently from a distance, while they will still secretly hold on to your connection, because they will never give up the pain that a situation created for two individuals. They have to blame something, because someone has to answer for the broken china plate that now rests in pieces on the floor.

Someone has to pay for the damages, someone has to clean up the mess, and someone should finally feel the hurt that you simply cannot feel -- which in the end makes me the most angry of all. They just want to watch you be tormented, because they secretly get pleasure in watching you struggle -- they think you had it so much easier than the road in which they traveled. They saw what life gave you from the start and think to themselves, "If I only had it that easy."

They may sleep at night, but they will never know the nightmares you experience when you both shut your doors for when the sun sets, and yet that poison still ruminates in their own tortured soul, "If I only had it that easy." You, and you alone, will become the reason why they still continue to walk down their lonely road of which they still wish to become of themselves. Their dreams will never die, and every small thing they accomplish, no matter how far away it is from their real dreams, they will act like it makes them happy on the inside, and they will lie to themselves every time they look at themselves in the mirror.

The reality is you have said you are sorry, but the one thing they simply cannot grow into has to remain a child for life, because they will never man enough to say to you, "There is nothing any apology you could ever say will remedy the situation that I had to endure, so I will go on the rest of my life, until the day I die trying to succeed by myself, when in my heart I know we could have made it as a team, but you made it this way, so you will be punished, and the only thing that gives me any joy anymore is knowing that I can still punish you."

Maybe one day before both your hearts will stop beating you may both come across the same thought which would heal a wound so big it will make all the warriors drop their arms, and all the healers shall pick up theirs, because "Wasn't this punishment enough?"

Functionless Filtration

There is a man who roams the land with an eternal curse, he believes he knows everything about those around him, the facts that he carries with him are but of limited knowledge, everyone knows not to tell him anything, because this man spouts words off his tongue without passing it through his brain; this is his tragedy with every spoken verse. He walks around with bright eyes and a smile wide, the people he calls friends are very limited, they are a rotating stock of people constantly getting burnt, and once you know his disability the information you will begin to hide. It will happen like clockwork on a daily basis, he will walk into a room of people and everyone changes their mode, his mouth will open and he will say something he thinks is witty and clever, his words will be offensive to someone's ear, and he will turn a party of conversations into dead silence and social stasis.

Everyone who holds whom he is as a person in an endearing light, those who know him well will hold what he hears quite distant, even the women who date him try their best to put up with his social retardation, but even he is dumb enough to say things that would make those who love him most put up a fight. Somewhere along his journey of growing up organically, he somehow got desensitized to what is right and wrong, his brain fires so fast with the ego that he can't seem to loose, and then he blurts out the last thing anyone wants to hear in a fashion that is designed mechanically. Some people find it humorous in the way it exists, it is not stupidity that causes it because he's extremely well read, he will go quite far in his educational realm, but there is no one stupid enough to make them his partner in business; his lack of filtration continually persists.

He will live his life always hating this lifestyle, when he makes a fool of himself on such a constant basis, the inner desire builds for him to prove himself to everyone else, his ego will be very delicate and you will always have to walk on eggshells regarding his feelings, and he will go his whole life making up for things he said; always left having to strive for that extra mile. Words are such a delicate thing in this society built on human conversation, everything you say to someone else psychologically affects them on some level or manner, this is a catastrophic social ailment as the chaos theory dictates eventually you will ignite a fire, and this is why he is doomed to have a life of endless frustration. To some degree we all know a functionless filter, it's extremely painful to watch, even more excruciating to live, this why all information needs to be held close to your mind, and never haphazardly spilled in a manner quite off-kilter.

Dipping Down

She's stuck on the roller coaster, and with each click she slowly climbs. She gets higher and higher over a gradual amount of time. After a certain point, she gets manic and loves every moment of life. Everything is moving so fast, everything is happy, and everything is so nice. She's capable of experiencing ten times any emotion you or I could feel, and because she's on such a high emotional frequency, she is often crushed by life's heel. As she climbs, her eyes get brighter; you can hear the joy in her voice.

When she hits her apex, there's only one place from there, she has no other chemical choice. As the final click of the uphill climb hits that point, that is when the cart she is riding in points downward, and quick! She comes blazing down at full speed, and, with each passing moment, she enters a state of greater and greater need. Like an asteroid that falls to the earth, she becomes filled with gloom instead of that bright, happy mirth.

She's traveling so fast, the cart she's riding almost seems it will be the last. She tries to brace for impact, but she is nowhere near the bottom, because she got so high before she will travel directly through summer and straight into autumn. Once she finally hits that low of all lows, she will cry on her bed just wanting to go. We all wish we were not on this ride that takes us through life, because it builds us up, and then causes us nothing but strife. What she needs to always remember, deep down in her core, no matter how low things may get – just like a Phoenix, she will once again soar.

She is one of the beautiful ones who can transmit her energy to others; but when she is low, she won't even bother. No matter the point you are in on the rollercoaster, just know that every emotion is part of the ride – and because of this gift you draw the best people in closer.

Manic Monster

It's just another day in your life and everything seems to be normal, then it will happen in a flash with the simple act of your brain firing, you will experience a chemical change in your mind, and then your quiet demeanor becomes something quite less than formal. Your eyes will grow wide, your thoughts will begin to race, your energy level peaks to something astronomical, and it's nothing you can hide. Your brain is working at full capacity, ideas sprout in your mind quicker than you can put them on paper, you think of things that are grandiose in nature, and your work ethic fills with tenacity.

In a flash you can't hold back your actions, you start frantically creating, you are looking at the norms and can't help but start deviating, and your energy is contagious which makes others want to follow you; no matter your faction. With an energy that is at full tilt, you frantically work on the ideas that come to your mind, nothing can stop you in this mode, and no one can cool you down because nothing causes you guilt. Some of the best things you have done in your life have been in this rare state, you only have a limited time to use this energy, you waste no time going to the drawing board, because you are fully-charged and this momentum cannot wait.

Others watch you in awe, they see what you have as a gift; you know with every high there will be an equal low, but you refuse to let that notion hinder your work, because you are about to make something that will create a big draw. Other great artists, painters, and musicians used this gift to create what we as a society deem as great, others will gather around you to watch your frantic process, and the people who will make money off your talent simply cannot wait.

Those who burn fast and hard, never live as long as the rest who keep a steady pace, the brightest lights burn out the quickest, and they are always the ones to play their best card. In the storm or fury and creation, they make something amazing for the masses to enjoy, every time they are finished they are drained and empty, the last thing they feel is pride for their work, they are not proud and there is no elation. After a long day of working their brains to the max, they drag themselves to their beds, exhausted in every possible way, and then they can isolate themselves and finally relax.

The next day you wake, the mania has finally subsided, you are a whole different person now, the insufferable monster comes out inside of you, and now your masterpiece is nothing more than something you want to destroy and break. You are your own worst enemy in every way achievable; everything you create becomes an undesirable entity to you, nothing satisfies you in your depressive state, and then you destroy yourself in ways not even conceivable.

You love the praise of others when you are high, the next day you are lower than low, you hate every moment of your existence, and all you want to do is die. You are on the rollercoaster of creating things new, you will make everyone who loves your work crave more, the emptiness you feel when you are low is so awful; the only color you can see is blue. There is a monster who lives inside of you, it can only temporarily be happy, the rest of the time you are sad, and everything you try to change in your life makes you realize there is no constant, and that's the only thing you can believe is true.

Most cannot last long with this condition, it drains your soul, it makes you emotionally flattened, and rarely it leaves you with any positive fruition. The majority of the afflicted choose to die young, whether it is a bullet to the brain, an overdose of pills that shuts down your liver, or the noose around your neck, which makes your mouth reveal a bloated purple tongue. The only thing you can do for these people is give them the applause they deserve, being a genius comes with a cost, they are only trying to make things in this short existence more beautiful, and as the viewer of such art validates them for their efforts, because your applause is the only way to properly observe.

Emotionally Empty

Vacant voids of listless eyes stare at reflections that no longer try, after flying to such a height and sinking to such a low you only can sigh, rather than a hello you would rather say goodbye, and you lose the ability to pull it all together to even apply. Everything that was sharp is now flat and dull, you don't even feel the chemicals that pass through your skull, and you have hit the soft ever-living null. You remember what it was like to feel such love, now the hand has outgrown the glove, and you just want your pulse to stop so you can ascend above. This is the apex of nothing and the low of everything that exists, the memories of the pain remain as scars on your wrists, and your feet still move one in front of the other because your life persists.

You can't even remember life's days that used to fill you with joy, now all you seem to want to do is slowly destroy, and this is what it is like when you are life's emotionless whipping boy. The silence of the empty room that is the only place you prefer to reside, long ago the passion that filled your soul has died, because now you are nothing inside. Life has become an unwrapped present, you are the brand new car with the giant dent, and when you can't feel anything at all it is the biggest torment. Your phone sits silent on the table when it used to ring, you are no more than a jester to please a king, and that person in the mirror is just a lifeless thing.

You are just a husk of organs that slowly decay, the dancer in a wheelchair at the ballet, and with each blow life delivers, you slowly lose your way. People who used to be friends don't even want to see your face, you did not have enough stamina to finish the race, and now you just orbit any feeling in outer space. You have become nothing but numb, the colors in your life are nothing but grey that is glum, and this emptiness will never leave you because this is what you have become. You are emotionally empty just like the rest, you don't even fight it anymore nor do you protest, and although your nerves may be working they are in a constant state of unrest.

Secluded Self-Sacrifice

In minds that contain uncommon patterns that the brain would not normally fire, the jugs of chemicals called brains that are statistically different in the chemicals that they store, and the ones worthy of the label "mentally ill" by a trained professional, which, if you ask the majority, is not something they would potentially desire. The fact remains that these beings don't fit in with the other members of society, they end up feeling like outcasts of everyone else, this is the reason why they become delusional and lose touch with their common brother, and these are the people who end up living very painful lives compared to other people who are considered the more common variety.

They know from the way the media portrays them, from how other people will turn away, the heavy stigma their existence carries with the others who believe that no deviations in thought or daily actions make you a better version of everyone else, and because they are the minority and unable to control themselves; low self-esteem begins to stem. This whole process of the machine in place makes them sacrifice their social lives, it becomes a vicious cycle, which only results in a circular procession of loneliness and unhappiness, and they lose all desire to fit in with everyone else and that causes no internal drives.

What can be done to help these people who feel they must seclude themselves in solitude, will a gesture of compassion be something that can cure this behavior, would education about the nature of their condition promote universal understanding, and will people do it in a way that isn't just an act of pity; would this help a multitude? They don't have the desire to be treated differently, they want some recognition of what sets them apart from the neurotypicals in life, because it is possible to show how you understand without using kid gloves incidentally. Spreading awareness that there is no real normality that is represented among the diversity of our breed, creating compassionate mindsets that will promote people to pick up one another when they fall down, and killing the archaic mentality that institutionalization is the general need.

The act of being discrete when you approach someone who is obviously having problems in their world, this will allow a comfort level between different types to be established, and then perhaps with their newly-formed bond they can straighten them out rather than watching them be tortured and curled. They are embarrassed enough that they need help, this is the reason why so many become homeless, because they would rather die in silence than admit that the system in place affects them so much they can't help but yelp.

If only people organically create opportunities that make it possible to educate, then we as a whole can share their perspective on the challenges they face with their diagnosis, and this would stop the trained behavior that has been since our evolution into what we are now which would be a knee-jerk reaction of discrimination. After this begins to take place, a shift of current viewpoints will finally take hold, because even though they are not both creating the same work output; both types of individuals will be a contributor to the common living space. There will no longer be those living in secluded self-sacrifice where the only social interaction they get is by looking in the mirror, people won't cross the street to avoid someone who obviously needs another's attention, finally the shroud of ignorance that plagues our mindsets will be gone, and because of this everyone will see things so much clearer.

Distantly Disassociated

After going to hell and back, I just sit on the floor staring at the carpet fibers on the in front of me. I begin to dissociate, and the carpet blurs into a solid color. My mind wanders, and I find myself thinking about all the people I have been ignoring my entire life as I searched for who I really was. The torment I endured for twenty-nine years was unspeakable. When you don't recognize yourself in the mirror, you begin to obsess about yourself nonstop – and that's all your life becomes. I'm afraid to look at my past social network posts because I don't even recognize my own writing. I wake up everyday with new folders on my computer, filled with messages for my future self.

After you have been everyone else, your inner voice just becomes the white noise to your life. I want to leave my flesh in the sink as I shower off the old me who used to exist. After realizing what you really are, you relive every moment when other people avoided you because they didn't want their existence "re-duplicated." The list of names grows to several pages, and you can't help but understand why they acted the way they did. Nice people included you because they saw your struggle – but even then, they couldn't tell you what you were because your ears would act as a firewall blocking out their words. The struggle is over, and you can't help but let in the emotion you have suppressed for decades.

Tears fill your eyes, and you cry without making a sound. You remember the one person who chose to be with you through your struggle, and then writhe in pain – as even she no longer responds to your messages. You can't blame anyone anymore as you slowly gain compassion for every living thing you encounter, because you have lived so many lives that you can't help but feel for everything with life in it. Even those whom you've avoided glide in and out of the picture, as your lip quivers with angst. Everyone else could see that picture, and now that you can too, you discover how someone you'd always criticized in the back of your mind was one of your closest friends; you feel like an asshole for being an elitist prick.

There was a point in time when you liked what you saw in the mirror, but that memory is so distant it makes your sadness even greater. Even now, the words just flow from your fingertips, and you don't know who's in control. Now you understand why you needed so much freedom and space – because you were such a big fish in a small habitat. The drugs you did were to only soothe you, as you took in every chemical available just to see if you could fix the broken machine. You reread the last sentence and realize that you

operate like something mechanical – rather than organic – and

suddenly, Kubrick's visions all make sense. You are your own worst

enemy, and you can't let it go. I sit here on the floor staring at the

carpet fibers in front of me.

They're There

Those who have the ability to dissociate are unable to be

harmed by the words or actions of other individuals. In fact, when

someone tries to hurt the feelings of someone who is dissociative,

those malicious efforts will only illicit joy, laughter, and mirth in that

individual. When you can dissociate the words of another human

being, it just becomes a psychological turn-on because you know that

you cannot be harmed. Instead you can destroy that individual

psychologically, dismiss them entirely, or give them such a high-

powered dosage of truth that you can render them inoperable.

Every human being has a mind like a lock; when you say the

right string of words to him or her, you can unlock them like a key

unlocks a door. Every being is searching for someone to unlock

them, because when you are constantly forced to be someone else in the society that you put yourself in, you are secretly looking for truth at every moment of your life. Every human being is being lied to 99% of the time; for that reason, we become "truth seekers." Those who can transmit truth to another individual have the power to make anyone gravitate towards them.

After you expose them to what is really going on, the person will first go into denial; but then, as they slowly accept the truth over time, they will come to you when they are ready, with tears in their eyes, because they are so grateful for escaping the lie they had been living their entire life. With the birth of the Internet, all truths are slowly being revealed to the masses, and not even faith can block out the actuality of what is really going on in this earth.

Forever Fearless

As a paranoid mental patient fear used to run my entire existence, I feared everything: the government, the police, my bosses at work, and even what people thought of me; the fear overcame my ability to function, no matter my daily persistence. Then one day I finally fought back, I told the thoughts in my head to fuck themselves, and from that moment I never looked back. I embraced the Omega and the concept of the end, it's such a beautiful thing if you think about it, I'd had enough of living in a state of impending doom, and from that moment in time I looked at Death as only my friend.

It's a miracle I am even typing these words, it's an anomaly that I even still exist, I tried committing suicide six times, while two of those times were cries for help, the other four were serious attempts at finally turning my brain off forever, because I no longer wanted to be with society or the herd. Now I live my life with no fear, nothing scares me, I'm friends with psychopaths, I write my thoughts without a fear that I will be black bagged by the CIA and taken away forever, I freed myself from the constant doom, and now to this day I only can cheer. You have heard it before, "There is nothing to fear but fear itself," escape those thoughts that anyone is out to get you, because you will live everyday like you will die tomorrow, and everyday you will get everything life has to offer and even more.

I am ready to die, I embrace the thought of some radical who hates my thoughts to come shoot me or stab me to death, I am free of the notion of wanting to live forever, and with this mindset I have grown wings and everywhere I go I fly. My breaking point of where I freed my paranoid mind happened in the Mojave Desert, I knew

what I had to do, and that was to be fearless in that sea of dirt. I am

afraid of the dark so to end all my fear I stripped down completely

naked only to be in my shoes, then I ran fearlessly into the dark

without a flashlight, I kept running and waiting at any moment that

something would emerge out of the darkness and tear me to shreds,

and after running for two miles nothing harmed me, and that

experience completely changed my views.

Now, wherever I am and where ever I go, I do every action

without fear, and because of this I truly live my life, and I have

everything to show. We innately want to preserve ourselves for as

long as humanly viable, it is human instinct to fear the unknown, and

we don't want to cross the line, because then we will be held liable.

Fear only keeps you in line and all you will do is stress, the key to life

is accept that you could die at any moment, and live a life that is

forever fearless.

Quantifying Quantum

The shift from one conscious realm and reality to another is a

mildly disorienting experience for the vessel that is going through the perception change of what their current world is presenting them as their determined existing environment. Moments ago I was in a reality that had so many different variables that were such a polar opposite to the one that I am currently now documenting this one in, that when there was that lightning flash that decided for an oscillation the dictated existing states my current reality, because I felt an undeniable cognitive buffering time that had to happen to acclimate me to my new surrounding environment before I could actually start existing in it.

When I perceived that the reality had changed from the previous one I was in, it took a defragmentation period that required a newly scanned packet of informational data to be collected from all five senses of my perception based reality determining sensors, and this process was to actually let my subconscious mind that was still expecting predetermined outcomes from the last conscious realm and reality to actually acclimate to this current reality that I am now existing in. We cannot start living in our current reality until both our conscious mind and subconscious mind synchronize in unification by the acclimation of data collected by the perception of our senses. Until one quantifies the surroundings of their environment they cannot start living in it, because they that will just

be expecting the preexisting variables of the information of their last

known encompassing perceived proximity.

SELF

Brilliance Beacon

He had many names and many forms, and not one word could ever describe his actions so we all just called him by his biological name that was passed down from his parents. One thing would be undeniably certain, whom ever he connected with in his life of surfing the societal seas, he would be a blinding light of truth, intelligence, and logic that makes all the dark spots in your perception that is dictating to you what you consider your reality crystal clear with a vibrational resonance that cuts through your internal doubt to heighten your conscious self-awareness of what power is actually subconsciously desired at the core of your being. He had the transmission that generated a key for any internal lock, once he opened me up I could never close myself again, and once I tuned in I never tuned out.

Absolute Attention

Born into a middle-class family he was an only child, with all the toys in the world, there was not a soul to share them with, no siblings to give him a sense of family, and this is why he became selfish with a sympathy that was mild. His energy was never-ending and massive like the sun, with desire he always strived to be the star, which was the center of everyone's constant attention, with parents who made him their focal point of every moment, because this is what becomes with love that should be for three children is all jammed into one. His parents stuck to him like masking tape, with a smothering mother and emotionally vacant father with no praise given, and this is the reason he always sought a sweet escape. He learned to adapt to his social surroundings at the drop of a dime, with a constant identity that would camouflage himself around others, because he could be whom he needed to with others in stealth; anywhere and anytime.

His father was intelligent and a self-made man who wore no real disguise, he always deviated from the societal norm, he showed calculation in every situation that would appear, and he always showed how he was wise. His expansive mind was always a growing root, he looked at himself in a higher regard, and he expected those in his life to follow suit. When it came to knowledge and clarity he was a treasure chest, everyone around him would always seek out advice, but when it came to showing affection to his offspring; he was as clueless as the rest. Little did he know about those times when he should have been an emotional man, when he would insist on pure intelligence to raise his breed, and that is why later in life this mistake would grow to be so uncontrollable it would ruin his life-long plan.

Then came his mother who monitored his every try, she never let him figure anything out on his own, which promotes a rebellious attitude at every turn, and she would follow the disasters he would create like an helicopter in the sky. With her obsessive eyes that could never turn away, her moods would fluctuate high and low, and she could never keep the other side of her from coming out; always trying to keep it at bay. His mother's weakness was emotional retention, the constant fixations of thought that her only one born needed her around the clock, and she overshot proper parenting by giving him too much attention. Perhaps for her there could have been a way, her son soon began to hate every moment he was forced with her presence, and perhaps there would have been a different organic path in both their lives; had she not smothered him throughout the day.

In the end, Mother's attention was unwanted, while Father's approval was misplaced, and together their presence in his life was nothing more than disgraced. That little boy would never entirely grow up at the end, when he looked in the mirror he saw a man who he did not know, this made him eternally empty inside because he had a hole he could never fill, he tried to bloat that void by seeking friends to have by his side, and gaining them through whichever means necessary; just to internally mend. He could speak anyone's language, gaining their trust, sharing their lives, he was greased up with charisma and he could slide into any wolf pack, and he sliced through those social barriers like the sharpest of knives. This wonder-boy was a newfound jack-of-all-trades, his voice split multiple ways with cunning and elation, which reflected his inner desire for always desiring acceptance and validation, and he could be the top of his class; even if he did not have the grades.

Forgotten Father

Prehistoric paternal patterns that are programmed intellectual elitists, they can only view things in a concrete state of scientific absolutism, and with every conscious effort they will strive for strategically deviating from any conventional mode of operation. With that heightened sense superiority that a prestigious college gives them with that piece of paper called a diploma, and their overblown ego with the inherit desire to fill the hole created by a lack of empathy due to an extreme emotional disconnect with the reality around them that a heightened intellect generates. With these flattened feelings they become emotionless robotic organisms, with every verbalized response that expresses feelings is a hollow vibration, and communication is no more than a preconceived string of dialogue that is generated in a desperate attempt to act like a human being.

They raise their young to be molds of perfection with validation that comes only when a job is done right, nothing is ever done right because they were not the one's that were in control, and so their children are only harshly criticized and lectured for every job they did not do well enough. After a while their offspring loses the desire of any appreciation of their father, the child will start to deviate from any level of power-generated life altering manipulation that is imposed, and the father will only show disproval with no affect that only brews an relentless anger from the lack of respect from his almighty force. When the father has to auto-correct the child's undesired behavior, since he is unable to feel emotions in the first place, will start wave after wave of pre-programmed intelligently verbalized emotional abuse tactically designed to hurt the most, and this is an attempt to control the child in a prison created by their ability to feel when he simply cannot.

As the years of this systematic pattern of intentional child defiance with the constant repercussions and exponential growth of the demands by the father, the repetitive and increasingly more vicious destruction of emotional wellbeing, self-worth, and self-esteem will continue, and this will drive the child to such a complete level of paternal apathy that they lose the desire to even see his own mortality. Due to the years of engrained emotional triggers and psychologically programmed emotional knee jerk responses, the tolerance level for the child to take emotional abuse has hit the wall where nothing the father says can impact them, by this time the he has resorted to every horrendous thing to say to abuse them, and despite the fact that no matter what he verbally concocts it is only a repetition which has no impact due to loss of gravity.

Then will come the point in time where both parties chose for a complete emotional, physical, and environmental separation, and they will both have such a tremendous amount of a negative ruminating vibrational frequency associated with one another that any future interactions will occur only due to the emotional obligation of another family member that brings them within a close proximity of each other. The father will grow ancient without ever accepting that the loss of his child was caused by anything that he did wrong, every time he stands in front of the mirror he will defiantly look past the reflection in the mirror, because if he really looked himself the visual echo of the sum of his manifested actions would make him feel something he had never felt before; self disgust.

Maternal Manipulator

The pure power and constant control that systematically stems from the apex of an alpha female, this woman will defiantly dominate even passive paternal protection, because she possesses an offspring obliterating obsessiveness that is fueled with the repulsive repetitive actions of a manically maternal manipulator. This is the only child that she will ever have, it is her one shot of obtaining a motherhood of memories, and with this awareness alone it only generates a fanatical focus that she will irreparably insist on sadistically smothering a continuously crying child. Every alarming activity will be declared a devoted dedication to the hopeless happiness of her child, the happiness of the child is dictated by a motherhood containing a multitude of moods that are managing the mother, and the mood of the mother is always determined on how tolerable the child is to such a confined and controlling parental power.

This worried woman is universally unable to take any form of constructive criticism, she must be absolutely right about anything, anywhere, and anytime, and this is the endless explanation behind why she has a preconditioned prestigious presence among any of her peers. These traits combined with the infinitive inability to accept that her constant cognitive creationism, because she will be nothing more than a fundamentally flawed forever. The mother that will primarily preconceive all social situations to a desirably definitive and determined outcome, because she must control all chaos while being continuously charismatic with every manipulative maternal moment.

This only causes personable people to be predominantly pushed away from her proximity, because with these atypically abundant absolutist actions they are always accustomed acts that appear to be nothing but simplistic socially synergy. There is no decent democracy in the loony land of the manic mother, she is the rule of pure power in a dangerously depressing dictatorship, and her gathered groups want to do nothing but leave the coop. Any insidious information that this wicked woman has on any private person or party will be an angst-ridden Achilles' heel of hurt, and will be nothing more than a weapon of war that can continuously be used angrily against them. Anyone who is lacking of fundamental finances will be no more than a personal puppet, and she will become their monetary master that constantly controls them.

In your youth every sadistic situation of mother's momentary malicious moods would taunt and turn terrible, and it always became nothing more than a child having to raise a child; the bigger of the two would always win. The woman that everyone would sadly see as your magical mother was nothing more than a warrior woman wearing two different mischievous masks, she could put on the maternal mask for the eye of the public, and then when the doors would close shut; out would come the mask of motherly malice.

Dating Duality

With a grin so wide it makes her uncontrollably reflect it, he lets loose a childish giggle with such a charismatic, animated, and playful tone, that it resonates in everyone within his proximity with the viral emotions that he will playfully transmit, and then he only magnetizes everyone in closer with his energy in that very second which his presence is publicly known. Across the room he can see a beauty in a midnight dress, she has a slender streamlined figure and a perfectly formed angelic face from which her sexual energy flows, his eyes narrow and shift focus and he suddenly changes into a whole new man with a silver tongue that is a social success, his art of seduction is mixed with a dangerously high intelligence and quick sensible wit and her level of intrigue only grows, because his presence becomes increasingly more powerful with a romance that makes with each tick in time more intense; with each passing moment he makes it harder for her to compose.

Like lovers on their honeymoon night he carefully carries her through her bedroom door, he gently rests her euphoria filled body on the soft silky fabric that is tight on her bed, she pulls him close by his tie and her teeth are sinking into her anticipating red lips because she only craves more, and with his large open hand he starts to stroke her soft thighs as both her legs twist and slowly spread. She can't help but release a slow primal moan that sounds like an alpha female from a wolf pack, when he hears this sound it makes him shift shapes into something uncontrollable and lusting with passion, articles of clothing are suddenly on the floor as she is pinned to the wall in dominance and all she can do is dig her nails in his back, and now she is powerless in such a sexual force of such an animal that even with the pain in the tremendous pleasure she can't deny the intensity of his compassion.

As her eyes open the next day to the aftermath of such intense desires that filled the entire night, the broken furniture that is on the floor in pieces and the articles of clothing that are all over the room, she looks for that creature that destroyed her in every right way and where it went she can only assume, but that beautiful darkness that made her feel so alive has sadly vanished in the rising sun's daylight. She huffs in grief as she accepts that she will never again experience such heightened pleasure again in her time, her body is still sore all over but those very aches she wishes she could feel anytime because she wants to recall such an incredible event, that two-headed creature was not only at it's sexual peak but also in it's passionate prime, as she lays on her bed that grin that she first saw last night organically grows on her face, his reflection is still inside her soul which is permanent like cement, and even though he has vanished his essence will never leave her place.

Death Drive

Ever since I was a child I loved to be the center of everyone's attention, I craved to be the center of everyone's universe, and I hope with every sentence that was spoken; I was someone that was worth a mention. As my mother's only child, I was the world to her, and because of this she would let me do anything; I was free to run completely wild. People always tell me what a big ego I present, that could be further from the truth, as I am empty inside, and the only ego that can be seen is when I am a puffer fish of energy, I will inflate to a certain size for a small period of time, and that only lasts until I have a mental chemistry change and then I am no longer along for the ride.

I find it hard to live with my existence, when I am put in a situation where I feel accepted by those with whom I am currently in the right social environment, I am a bright shining beacon of positive human energy, and any time I am not, I will keep myself isolated and at the furthest distance. What drives this vessel that is an energy battery, I am driven on nothing but positive verbal reinforcement, when I am not feeling the love of others, I will often crash on someone's negative vibe, and that causes me to end up in a depressive downward spiral, and then others have to mediate with ego-boosting tactics; nothing but pure validation and reinforcement.

The phoenix will burst into flames in times of rejection, what ultimately kills the core of my being, what shuts me down entirely is the pain of human silence, and it is the cycle of my life which is the constant yearning for human affection. When I am ignored, it leads to paranoia, I feel more alone than ever, I become the outcast filled with social despair, and then I will isolate myself and feed off the pain of loneliness, which leads me sad and bored. Romantic entanglement for such a being is a near impossibility, love me too much and your obtainability becomes a turn-off, love me too little and I will obsess over your every action, because of this I am confined in a state of despair in an undesirable facility.

I am the boy who is looking for the woman with a high material desire, it is a twisted desire but there are many out there who would dream of such a man, but they are as twisted as I am, and because of this there can be no internal passion that leads to fire. The insane want someone sane to be their lover so they can be grounded, opposites attract for a reason because we are looking for someone who has what we don't have ourselves, once in a great blue moon a couple like this finds each other, but because of the stored up loneliness for so may years in solitude one only gets turned off because they are obsessively hounded.

The boy will be filled with anger one moment as he creates a scene, then the desire to be molested by his lover on many levels, and after the intimacy he is back to treating her like a queen. With sex always on the brain, he always speaks before he thinks, he has no filter and no ability to restrain. At times when the chemical imbalance makes one feel incredibly low, they have the desire to shrink back to the size of a baby so they can reenter the womb, all so they don't have to have the responsibilities that crush them in live be put to an end, so they no longer have to put on a show.

The womb was filled with a carefree, protective, and warm place, it was before the time when all the pain in life started, you won't have to look in the mirror everyday at that person who you just don't want to be, because you just can't handle the sight of your face. The daily routine of adulthood becomes so heavy on the human soul, you are on a daily basis pushed to the limits of what you can tolerate, sometimes you would rather die than fill out more corporate paperwork, and you wish that there was a place for everyone who can stand the burden to just crawl into an eternal hole.

You will never reproduce because you cannot develop past a certain mindset, you are trapped as an eternal child, and you don't have the abilities to enjoy all the fruits of recreation, because all it would bring are more responsibilities that would make you endlessly fret. Money is the last thing you ever worry about, it's not like material possessions will turn your life around from what it is now, and the only thing you can do is shove your head in the pillow while you cry and shout.

Your interests have never evolved past things that give you instantaneous gratification; only intelligence in another individual makes you seldom want to be intimate with a lover, your hormones that drive the masses are void from your system, you don't crave the flesh, the touch, or a temporary release, all you seem to care about is what you want to do and your own personal satisfaction. You have a drive that seldom endure while they are alive, you are ready for the end of life, and you are stuck in a pattern with nothing more than a death drive.

Screaming Silence

The universe that was created inside your brain, it was designed to distract you from the past trauma you endured, because of your never-ending emotional pain. Everything finally comes full circle in a monumental moment of total clarity, there is nothing left that can be fabricated to distract you from your past, and you reached complete self-awareness; for most, it is a rarity. Every action you ever made becomes painfully clear, the people with whom you chose to associate, and the ones whom you deemed worthy enough to keep near.

You understand why others looked at you with eyes that would judge, the people who knew what you were chose to be distant, and you can't help but understand the reason for their actions; you hold no grudge. The whispers about you when people thought you were out of earshot, the delicate manipulation others would use for their own personal gain, and after taking all of this in and accepting it you just want your stream of running consciousness to shut off and never have another thought.

The reality of what you are cannot be blocked out, you want to tear your skin off, and you wish that you were anything else; there is no other route. Crippling anxiety shoots through your core, you gasp for air as your lungs feel crushed, and with each moment that passes the incredible angst you feel becomes more and more. Knowing that everyone else could see what you were, you were blissfully ignorant for such a long period of time, and there were those who were kind enough to hold a mirror up to your essence; all you could see was a blur. You are nothing more than a collection of people you deemed to consciously copy, you are nothing more than a husk that collects personalities, and now that you accept that you can't identify yourself with anything; your mental waters nothing but choppy.

You may feel like human duplication, just a clone of what others made you feel you wanted out of life, because you admired another's conscious fabrication. The reality of the situation is you are nothing more than an adaptable entity, where others do not have the ability to be malleable in life, yet you are special because you can mesh with any group of society. Feelings may arise where you are just a drone of what others psychologically expect from your behavior, you are not one thing, rather, everything, and this adaptable trait can often be your savior. If you become stagnated by your surroundings, know that you can shape shift, know in the back of your mind that you have the freedom to go anywhere, and the pain you once endured created a tremendous gift. When the screaming silence of knowing what you are prevents you from being able to function, remind yourself that you

have the power to change your reality, and you will no longer feel like a being considered a malfunction.

Calculating Consciousness

It's the running voice you hear when you are awake. It tries to make everything real around you when, in reality, it's fake. It's every memory you have ever had, and it tries to keep away the feelings that were once bad. It paints a pretty picture in color when everything is just black-and-white. It is nothing more than a giant electrical storm in your brain. It makes you cling onto life even when you harbor disdain. Your associations of the past fuel your choices, all the way down to your dendrites. Those associations dictate you, through your programmed morals, in what becomes your version of wrong or right.

Your consciousness has the ability to expand, to reach higher limits, to fully understand your fellow man. This program running in your brain determines whether you choose to be good, evil, or neutral in this world where there is always something to gain. Your consciousness can become peaceful, or your consciousness can become deadly. Your consciousness can dominate, or your consciousness can become as passive as a dinner plate. What happens when your consciousness splits into two, and you are given two options in life between which you are forced to choose? Which do you pick: A or B? When your consciousness splits off like the roots of a tree, you seem to want everything – because that's the only way you can seem to be.

Two minds thinking in one brain; with this set of circumstances, how is one supposed to sustain? How does one act in this condition? Does he or she only display one mindset for continuity, or do you reveal yourself to the masses as some type of oddity? When you have the ability to adapt to any surrounding, where are your feet? Where do you hold your grounding? What it really boils down to is that you just have to force yourself to fit in, even though you hate constantly changing the shape of your skin. Some people use this skill to their advantage; they are civilians by day, and madmen by night.

You want to be inactive, but at a moment's notice you want to join the fight. You no longer see that happy child in the mirror anymore; rather, something that has grown into the unknown. With each passing day, you morph into something else. You begin to multiply with each person you meet, picking up their positive traits while you shake hands and greet. What is your label when you are nothing and everything at once? People only doubted your potential because of what they could not see at that very minute; then, you prove them wrong by pulling off your mask and showing them that you are in it to win it. The thing about gold medals is that their novelty slowly wears off, then, that prize you achieved collects dust as the notion of it only makes you scoff. The ability to think is the curse; emotionless masses converse.

Boyish Beliefs

When time froze and you were faced with a situation you thought would bring doom, someone inside you came to your rescue to save you from your peril and gloom, and since that moment he has always been there; you wear him like a costume. You would always be stuck in that mindset as a boy, no matter how much you aged as a person he would be ready to deploy, and although you pretend to be normal to the faces who know you; there are two of you and one is a decoy. Society is no place for a child's mind, there are many evils in the world that are quite unkind, and he always has to guide you; you are combined.

You will always like the things that make you feel young, whether it is fireworks, squirt guns, toy stores, or dirt that can be flung, and it is why you have the urge to be juvenile with words on your tongue. Everything you know is just a simplified explanation of how things will work, it is the reason why you get joy out of the misery of others with an immature smirk, and it is the reason why you are quick to argue when you are wrong in a situation that is knee-jerk. You stay up into the late hours because now you finally can, you disobey others wishes because you like to deviate from the dictated plan, and every time you look in the mirror you never see the reflection of a man.

Every time this child in you comes out he makes a mess, the other version is always forced to clean up, apologize, and confess, and it is because of this duality that creates so much endless stress. The women you date are all maternal in a nature defined, they are screwing a man who is difficult and cleaning up after a child's state of mind, and they are essentially another version of your mother who you had to find. Your boyish beliefs will never leave the thing that you are, you need attention constantly but you keep those whom you love distant and far, and this whole lifestyle you live is what makes you so bizarre.

Morbid Metamorphosis

Some individuals have a very dark, voracious entity dwelling deep inside them that is always observing the reality around their proximity. These people are generally the most kind, empathetic, loving individuals you could ever meet. They will bend over backwards to help those in need, they are humanitarians, and they accept everyone that walks this earth, because they understand how everyone is just a victim of circumstance. The search for people in pain, and will try to do anything at their disposal to help them. They have an internal need to help others in distress and grief, because they themselves are experiencing some kind of emotional trauma.

They see the people around them in society as brothers and sisters, and will stop any required obligation of them so they can help those who need it. They are angels who walk among us, and they are selfless in every aspect. The opposite sex is generally attracted to these wonderful people, they find comfort in their presence, and generally they desire to produce offspring with these pure souls. There is no denying that chaos exists, and no matter how safe you feel there is always that factor of a very awful situation arising. When these people are confronted with a potentially dangerous situation it's not the aggressor who is in control, in fact it is quite the opposite.

When put in a dire situation where these people who are generally beams of light of a perfect human being feel ill-at-ease, an instantaneous metamorphosis will happen. Their eyes will turn into dark voids, their heads will lower, and a voice that is very deep and dark will send out a booming command. Whether these, human threats, miscreants, or dregs of society have a weapon or not it is of no concern to these people. They do not fear death, because they embrace it. In life, the agony of having to contain a demon inside of them makes them among the most vicious beings on the planet. Generally, if the entity posing danger to them is smart enough, it will vacate the area just by the radical change in its voice, but if it chooses to stay and perform the nefarious deed that it preconceived there will be a harsh lesson that it will never forget.

These people who transform are not insane, rather, they just have no fear, because what they just turned into is a defense

mechanism of their consciousness, and no amount of pain and

suffering will prevent them from obliterating the threat that is

confronting them. This force they have turned into is one of the

most

lethal of our universe, and it will stop at nothing to ensure the safety

of its loved ones. When the threat is gone it will resume the shape of

the beautiful person it once was, and everyone can go home. It

should raise serious questions in one's mind. Is it worth it to commit

a petty crime, or have a bloodthirsty demon

come out of someone who appears to be normal, only to be left

eviscerated on the street screaming for any sort of medical

assistance? If this sounds like a fairytale to prevent crime I would

greatly consider what just wrote this piece.

Observing Overlord

He waits in the background of your mind – viewing

everything you experience, and he bides his time. Constantly

observing, analyzing everything, only few know what he is about –

and he is waiting for the perfect moment to come out. He directs, he

protects, and he defects. Like a monster inside you, just waiting to be released – his presence will be with you until you are deceased. In times of trouble, he instantly snaps into action; he becomes you, and your tongue speaks his every intended action.

He is unstoppable, he commands – and others listen to his demands. He rarely surfaces – only rare instances bring him outside; other than that, he is just along for the ride. He is the dark passenger of my life; he is devious, and he will stand for no strife. He is my internal defender, and I have had him for as long as I can remember. He guides me, he thrives me, he makes me whole; but having him with me carries a toll.

I harbor two different souls in this organic structure; without him, I am nothing but a shell, a husk of man – because he's the only one who dictates the plan. I would be lost without him, I would not know what to do; there is a split in my consciousness – and no matter what, I cannot break through. Together, we have different tastes: I like ice cream, and he likes cake. He desires sex, but I desire intellect.

He manipulates those around him, whereas I only show love to them. I wake up everyday to new folders on my computer that I don't remember making; he writes, creates, and some of his work leaves me shaking. I've asked myself a thousand times, "What the fuck am I?" His reply is, "Nothing."

He is a charmer, a master of speech, and a societal leech. It's tough balancing out the things he will do; but I have to correct it, I must follow through. It's hard being both the yin and the yang; I try reminding myself we are just one, but it's tough to ignore him when he just wants to have fun. He is an expert at shooting me in the foot – a master of self-sabotage, we hate each other; but I have to accept him because he is my internal brother.

People who know me personally know there are two sides to this coin; the only problem is, it never lands on heads or tails – I wish the two would just join as one. The two sides are just constantly in the air spinning – and, unfortunately, no side is winning.

B Begins

When I was just a child, around the age of three or four, something extremely horrific happened, something so awful and traumatic my consciousness could not deal with it. When your consciousness can't deal with the current reality, something amazing happens, because during that magnitude of stress and pain, your consciousness rips in half. You, at that moment of horror, split in half as a person, and another consciousness develops to protect your current consciousness.

There becomes Consciousness A, the one whom you had been living your whole life experiencing, and then out stems Consciousness B to protect you from any dire situation. "A" is your personality that everyone knows, loves, and thinks of when they think of "you," and "B" remains dormant in the background constantly narrating everything that it is witnessing. "B" has a mind of its own.

It thinks of everything you wouldn't think of, and you can sit in your head all day long arguing back and fourth, debating between "A" and "B." You are not "he or she." You are a "we." Together you are one, and together you form two completely different functions as one individual. "A" handles everything that's cheerful and delightful about life, and then when "the shit hits the fan" out comes "B" ready to fight like something primal and visceral.

Sometimes you will be "A" and then someone will say something in your day-to-day life, and then out pops "B" with a venomous tongue with toxicity so acidic it burns through everything it touches. "B" is a cold, calculated, reptilian, and machine-like entity, whereas "A," on the other hand, is nothing but the delight of humanity. I lived twenty-six years of my life not knowing I had both "A" and "B" inside me. Sure, I would switch on people, and people would think, "Who the fuck was that guy/thing?" How do you as a friend approach someone and say, "Hey, I think there might be two of you inside that noggin of yours?"

I was just a drug-addicted filmmaker enjoying my life of doing jack-shit. I would smoke weed everyday, masturbate, fuck around on my computer making music, and then I would shower and go to sleep. Then I found LSD. I had screwed around with acid a few years back when I had a psychological breakthrough in San Francisco. Thanks to some trusted friends, some spirit guides, I had realized I was many different personalities living in one body. I soaked up whatever I liked about other people and turned that into my universal singular personality. I had no clue about "A" or "B."

A few nights previous I had done some LSD and spent the entire trip by myself undergoing some personal exploration, which is a big no-no if you ever do acid. I was sitting on my bed watching the fan spin above me. There was something fun about watching that fan, it had some screws loose or something so when it spun around it did so kind of chaotically, so you never knew when would be the last rotation before the whole thing would come apart and come crashing down all over the room. It was quite entertaining. It was cold in that old house, so naturally I had the fireplace going, and it was at a full roar.

Now, I am not religious. I do not believe in God, other than God being love, and I certainly don't believe in the devil. There is no red man with a pitchfork tempting us to do wrong, I am no fool, I read my Nietzsche, and I know what idiotic tools of brainwashing "Good" and "Evil" are. There is only what is right to do as a human being, and what is wrong to do as a human being. Suddenly, it happened. Now, one can view what I am about to tell you three ways:

1.) The devil was talking to me. The almighty Satan was choosing me as a vessel to do his dirty work.

2.) As a mental patient I was having a "command hallucination," which was probably brought on by the recent amount of LSD usage that had built itself up in my cranium.

3.) *This is what I personally believe.* I believe that "B" was tired of being a constant passenger in my life, and for once in his/it's existence, it wanted to be recognized, and it wanted me to acknowledge its power.

I was staring at the fan, and suddenly, I hear in a voice that was deep, powerful, and several octaves lower than anything I could produce as a trained voice actor: "ZACHARY." I instantaneously jumped up from the bed, looking around in all directions for the source of that voice. Was someone in my house? Who had a voice so commanding and powerful? What the FUCK was that? "ZACHARY, WALK OVER TO THE FIREPLACE." I was so scared, at this point, my whole body began trembling. I slowly put one foot on the floor, just to see if I could feel the ground beneath me, because everything seemed so unreal. I slid my other foot onto the floor and stood upright.

It boasted again, "COME OVER TO THE FIREPLACE." I slowly, with each apprehensive step, walked over to the fireplace. As I slowly made my way over to the fireplace, my eyes darted all around the room; I could have sworn I had felt someone else there with me, as if there was another unseen presence with me. I looked into the fire and what I saw was like nothing I had ever seen fire do before. It

was entrancing, the way it danced, the way it moved, I was sucked

into it, it had my full attention, and I slowly walked over to the

fireplace and sat down on the warm bricks that outlined the visual

display in front of me. I finally felt a bit of courage, and I spoke with

no one in the room to the fire, "Whaaa, what do you want?" I must

have looked like a madman from a fly-on-the-wall's perspective. I

was mad, I was completely and utterly insane in every way.

It commanded again: "I WANT YOU TO SUBMIT." I couldn't

believe what I was hearing, I was staring into these flames and I was

hearing that they wanted me to submit. I didn't even know what that

meant. Submit to what? Submit to whom? Another question

popped in my mind, why in the fuck was it calling me "Zachary?"

Only close friends call me "Zachary," and even then, they don't even

call me that, they call me "Zach." It repeated itself, only much louder

this time: "I WANT YOU TO SUBMIT!" What could I say? I was

staring at a talking fire that wanted me to submit to it. How often

does that happen in your life? What if I denied it of what it wanted?

What if I ran away screaming, and called the police, telling them, "My

fireplace is talking to me, and it wants me to submit!" With a great reluctance, I was about to do what it asked: "SUBMIT!" It beckoned me one final time, and then, with every part of my body, spirit, and essence, every part of me submitted to the fire. I submitted. I gave in. Then, suddenly, I snapped out of the fire's trance, stood up with zeal, and walked calmly back to my bed.

For years I never told anyone that story. I didn't want to hear any of that "You are possessed by the devil" bullshit. About a week ago, I was talking to my therapist, a nice woman, who doesn't believe in any of that religious nonsense, and having her know that I was (mis)diagnosed as an schizoaffective; I finally told her the story. "That was just a 'command hallucination.'" I nodded, "Yeah, you are probably right."

After going home and psychoanalyzing the entirety of the situation, I realized that that was no hallucination at all. That was "B" finally coming out, saying he exists inside me, and that I need to listen to him, because he knows what he's talking about. That was the night that "B" escaped, and since that moment, we have been working as a team. Who do you think wrote this whole story? We did.

Separated Sponges

After the two versions of you accept each other's existence,
you can't deny the fact that each version of you has different desires
in the world you both live in, and even though you argue back and
fourth in your mind as to which choices should be made in life there
always seems to be the inner struggle of resistance. You both
slowly accept that you no longer have to pick up the traits of other
people whom you both consciously admire, and you just want to
cleanse yourself of all adopted personality traits, and choose a
lifestyle to which you both actually aspire. You have been collecting
the best identities you could find in society, but after the awareness
of your actions you suddenly want to choose things to be your
desired variety. There is no longer the pressure to soak up what you
deem admirable from any other human being, since you have lived
this way your whole life to adapt, and you find the notion of
dropping your expected social role nothing more than freeing.

A life of constantly altering your internal mindset to please
those in your proximity, the bile rises in your stomach as you realize
how you were forcing yourself to adapt to every situation, and you
have become nothing more than a drone with a cognitive process of
one with unanimity. You would produce random oscillating

conscious variations, once a skeleton key into any door of society,

but now all you desire is only one plastic mindset because you can

no longer take

the constant psychological rotations. All you desire now is a

detoxification of every identity, you want solitude and silence as you

purge every entity you collected, and you pray that you can slowly

become your own entity. Shape shifting on a daily basis may have

allowed you to see things others never will, but for now the novelty

is over and you no longer want the thrill.

Now that you have accepted what you are, you can consciously

choose your own path of life, because chasing other's desires only

distances yourself until the person you see in the mirror is only

remote and far. You no longer have to eat what others find pleasing

to the tastes of their palate, no longer do you have to be a consumer

to the products that others choose, because now, for once in your

life, you can cast your own ballot. By accepting that you can be

anything you want in this universe, accepting that you were just

following the pack makes you realize you had no identity of your

own, and that feeling alone makes you feel nothing more than a

drone that was perverse. With the gift of self-awareness you can be

a separated sponge, you can choose things that really make you happy, and the only thing left for

you to do now is walk to that ledge and take the final plunge.

Conscious Clocks

Shifting conscious entities as you part the societal seas, as a
blender of thoughts the only thing that grounds you is the elemental
organic structure of your knees. As you collect, connect, and defect
from every sect you strategically move through every parsec.
Shifting masks to do required tasks as you look for a source of
warmth that will hold long enough for you to bask. Holding your
breath for others as you make room for your brothers without
mothers. The weight of another reminds you of your own, but it
does not give your empty echo anything but a reflective tone. A
ghost in some rooms and a god in others, epic events may collect in
your veins, but in the rain your internal fire only smothers.

Your light may teach the dumb, but your darkness only makes
you numb, as you try to hold a shape to a power that beats to its own
drum. The empathetic scream of the horrors of another fills every
vivid dream as with each new day you churn the common goals into
something everyone can openly beam into the pulse of the stream.

You make the miscreants wonder and the immoral weak as you alter the preexisting notions of what others consider the peak. When the universal conscious enlightenment finally ticks on the master's clock, the predetermined sequence of power-fueled emotions used to be the matters that bound us in plastic conditions, but now every number will have no meaning even if those who choose to control it by counting the finical stock.

Other's Oblivion

Everyday when I wake up I just sit in bed, I am filled with fear and a sense of impending doom, I try to gather the strength to get up onto my feet, as I am still groggy from the anti-psychotics I took the previous night, I try an familiarize myself with my current surroundings, and I try and find some normality in my head. I go to the coffee machine and make myself a cup, I take a few stimulants to give me inner strength, and sit in one spot as I slowly wake up.

I will go to my phone, there will be messages from names that I don't recognize, and people that the other guy was romancing the night before; I have to read through the messages to see what he had said so I can synchronize our personalities, because if I don't those people will be no more than unknown. I walk over to my computer to see the work he had done the night before, my computer is filled with new folders, new writings, and posts on social networks; every time there is brilliance that he wrote, and other times there are horrific posts that I have to quickly delete and there are never just a few things rather a whole lot more.

Everyday when I am, what I think what personality is me, I try and create nothing but beautiful things for others to see. When he takes over, he is nothing more than a sadistic man, he will destroy my image that I want to portray to the masses, and he goes to no limit to defile every thing I want to exist, and he destroys every single plan. Every few days I am left with nothing but a mess to clean up, I have to correct his actions, apologize to my friends, try and rebuild burnt bridges, and I can't help but look at this situation as a half-full cup.

Others who know me well enough know when he has taken over, some people quite like him because he is charismatic, witty, sharp, and tactical, but living with him is no four-leaf clover. It's no blessing being two people in the same husk, we are loved by many; a caring individual who only wants the best for people by day, and then you change into a monster by the time it hits dusk. Every medical professional always says it's all in your head, people of a different philosophy tell you to meditate and find your Zen, they don't understand the process how you have retrograde amnesia every time you wake up in your bed.

I am forced to live the life of taking responsibility of every action, because I am just one man, you can't blame something that lives inside you, this makes you live a life of constant apologies, and you never get validated and there is never any satisfaction. You become nothing more than a psychological oddity, everyone wants a peek at the man who is two people, and in this capitalistic society you are nothing more than a marketable commodity. Humans fear the unknown, when you admit to them what you really are, you are left at arm's length at all times, and the loneliness of those who don't understand you only makes you let out a painful groan. You wish you had a different evolutionary trait like the ability to fly, but these were the cards you were dealt, and you are only left with the other guy.

Collecting Collectives

We or I am nothing more than a collection of personalities that I have met as I have lived on this Earth, my consciousness is a selective entity, and I only adopt those people who bring to this world mirth. I only adopt the positive traits in people who I meet, they have to have a worthy persona, when I find someone who is worthy of impersonation, I will soak them up like a human sponge, then when they leave my presence I transform into them, and then I move on to the next social circle in which I will enthusiastically greet. I am a collective of everyone who was ever great, I can merge into any social circle, take on any role that I need to fill, and I have no identity of my own; I only display a happy image and I rarely hate.

When you can become everyone, you learn all the different walks of life; you can't judge anyone, because at one point you have lived that way, you are every number and you are also none. Everyone who knows me in the society that I mesh in, they have a different expectation of how I will act in front of them, none of them know it's just a reflection of others who I have met, and because of this I never lose and always win. It becomes problematic when I am forced into a group setting, when the multiple people I am duplicating are in the same proximity, I will have to merge identities, that can be quite revealing leading others to a state of confusion, and I am always careful in how I act because I don't know who to be; which leads me sweating.

Everyone has this trait, not to the extent of my life, but you become who you associate with no matter the setting, the mindset of the group will dictate your behavior, and when you are around bad people you become someone who makes choices that are not so great. Why be forced into living a life where you don't make the choices of what you want to do, you are just following the pack mentality, and you will have no sense of who. Everyone in society is nothing more than a collective collection, now that you know this, think about who you really want to be, because you can always change who or what you are, and you can put yourself in a different section.

Total Trip

I was always a social surfer. In high school, I was a human chameleon – I belonged to five different social circles, and every day of the week I would visit each social circle. The different circles provided my soul with different mindsets. I was collecting the personalities of these different individuals in these groups. I hung out with the science dorks, I hung out with the skater kids, I hung out with the jocks, I hung out with outcasts, and I hung out with cool kids.

Each circle provided me with different personality traits to adopt, which made me a whole human being. I was nothing but a husk, searching for people with positive qualities who my consciousness found deeming of impersonation in other situations where those individuals were not present. My closet was nothing more than a wardrobe of different costumes. I would change costumes for each social circle I was a part of, so that I would be accepted. You have to look like a lamb to walk with the sheep.

Then, two of the smartest people I knew picked up on this behavior; they were in the scientist circle. They noticed the organism who I was. Constantly changing, constantly evolving, constantly shape shifting. Moe, one of the scientists, would always drop comments – that he was onto my behavior, and that he knew what I was. When someone says something so specific, so geared to who you are as a spirit – it instantly grabs your attention, and you know exactly what he or she means with one short, calculated sentence.

I went on with this behavior, despite being recognized. It was the only way I knew how to live – and the system worked well for me, so why fix a machine that is not broken? Then came college. I knew filmmakers, and I was a very funny guy – that's how I fit into every social circle to begin with. I was the comedian, and everyone loves a comedian. Everyone loves the jokester, the trickster, and the fool. I followed the exact lifestyle of one filmmaker named Eddie. Eddie had his shit together. He knew what he was doing.

I wanted to be Eddie, so I became him – in every way possible. Of course I would deviate in aspects where he could not see his own flaws, because I wanted to be flawless. After almost finishing film school, I found a job at a local Internet television studio, and I became their golden boy. I could morph into anything they wanted, I could write anything they wanted. I could act, just as I had been acting my entire life – so, by this point, I was a professional. Then, I convinced the executives of my genius, and they gave me my own web series – which I created, directed, and acted in.

It was all improvised – with only key story points to keep the plot moving to make it an actual, watchable show. After the final fourteenth episode, I was a star. People around Las Vegas would say,

"Hey, aren't you that guy from that show?" I felt god-like; I had created something that everyone loved, and I was using a collection of personalities I had gathered to do so. I had models on the show, personalities from popular radio stations, famous people, and I was a rock star – and I loved every minute of it. Then, Moe came out of the woodwork after seeing my success as a writer and actor.

Moe played a very specific role in my life. He guided me with his carefully-placed words, and he was my spiritual shaman. I never once ignored anything he had to say. Then, one day, Moe introduced me to a friend who had been watching me from the sidelines – his name was Jack. Jack was also a genius. He was an engineer and he had recently been hired by NASA. Moe, on the other hand, majored in biochemistry – and then began to create new medicine for pharmaceutical companies.

They were both geniuses and they saw my inner torment; they had watched me grow through high school, they had watched me grow as a filmmaker, and they knew who WE really were. I am a master manipulator of every situation, because I adapt to every situation and always make things go my way. Moe and Jack combined figured out a way to scientifically manipulate the manipulator – for which I give them credit, because they did an outstanding job. Moe had moved to San Francisco and was a part of the scientific revolution that had started there. He worked at a laboratory, and he knew organic chemists.

Organic chemists know how to make the most powerful thing on this planet – and little did I know what would be in store for me. That's when the brainwashing commenced. Moe, one day, out of the blue, started talking about LSD. What a fantastic creation it was. The amazing powers that it had. "Zachary, you are an amazing artist. Do you know what happened to the Beatles after they dropped acid? They started making music that changed the world. Don't you want to harness that power? Don't you want to change the world?"

I did want to change the world. I personally believed I was something fantastic, and yes, indeed, changing humanity seemed like a worthy thing – a noble cause. The seed was planted. Moe then called my parents and said, "Hey, you know, we have noticed that Zachary has gotten into a funk; he bought that Glock 9mm and that Ak-47 with a 75 round drum attachment. Doesn't that stockpiling mentality worry you?" I was in a state of paranoia; I didn't know who might be out to get me, but I was ready to battle to the death with any aggressors who were out to harm me. This was during the Bush Era, so paranoia was already running high in my blood.

I was ready for a revolution. It was Orwell's worst nightmare I was living in, and there was no goddamned way I wasn't going out with an extended fight. I was a gamer in high school – I played the computer game "Counter Strike," and I was damn good at it. I was tactical and deadly. If there was one thing that was certain, in my mind, it was that, in the end, my kill/death ratio would be thirty-six to one. I was a fucking warrior prepped for battle. Moe convinced my parents that a group of old high school friends were meeting up in San Francisco, and that it would do me a world of good to see all these old familiar faces.

Sure enough, my parents purchased me that plane ticket to go on a little "trip." After hearing that my parents were flying me out to San Francisco to see my old friends, I entered a state of mania – and that seed that Moe had planted blossomed. I told Moe, "Look, man, I don't care who you have to talk to, who you have to go to, but get some fucking LSD so I can evolve. I need this, I really do." I could hear the smile in his voice: "Yes, Zachary, I most certainly will; in fact, I know just the chemist to get it from so it will be very pure."

Moe was determined that I make the trip – so he even assigned a guy named Jeff, with whom I had always shared a mutual dislike, to babysit me and fly with me so I would make the journey. It was all part of the plan. After arriving in San Francisco, we landed and we all went back to Moe's place. There were four of us: Jack had flown down from Texas, leaving his job at NASA to come for this masterfully-planned event; Shaun, a neutral party; Jeff, the antagonist; and myself. We planned to drop the LSD in the morning, so we all hit our beds early that night to prepare for the event that would monumentally unfold the next day.

Once I awoke the next day, everything got weird. Everything was happening like clockwork; things were too calculated. Everyone was in on the same plan – except for me. Shaun and Jeff left for the day to go to the park, because they wanted to have nothing to do with the drugs; and then, Moe's girlfriend, Valerie, came over with a notepad and a pen so she could "babysit" us and document everything she would see unfold. "Are you ready, Zachary?"..."Fuck yes!" I said, in a state of mania.

The LSD was kept in the freezer to preserve it – to make sure there was not a single flaw in the scientific process that was about to

unfold. It was wrapped in tinfoil, and each of us – Moe, Jack, and I –
all picked up that sugar cube filled with the knowledge of the
universe inside it, and we placed it in our hands. "Let's go outside;
it's such a beautiful day," Moe said. We all walked outside. We all sat
around a circular table – except for Valerie, who sat on the sidelines,
getting ready to write and document what she would see unravel in
front of her.

      "We all ready?" Moe asked. We all answered with a gleeful
and unanimous, "Yes!" That's when we all placed the sugar cubes
into our mouths; the sugar slowly dissolved, and the LSD was
dispersed into our systems. About twenty minutes passed, and then
I uncontrollably laughed like a maniac and yelled in a voice I had
never heard come out of my body before, "This shirt is too
confining!" I took my shirt off, and threw it to the floor. Moe handed
me a piece of paper and said, "Why don't you make a paper airplane,
Zachary?" I instantaneously replied, "Have Jack do it – he's the one
who works for NASA." We all shared a laugh filled with mania.

      Then, it happened. I felt a chemical change in my brain – a
flood of chemicals shifting from one side to the other. Neurons were
firing differently, and then I said something profound, prolific, and it

grabbed everyone's attention immediately. Valerie instantly wrote it down. Moe and Jack then looked at each other and both nodded. It was time. The LSD had kicked in, and now was the time for their master plan that they had orchestrated. "Zachary, it's getting hot outside; let's go into my room for a minute."

At this point, I was just a human puppet. I pulled off my gym shorts because they were bothering me, and then I walked into Moe's room with Jack following me as I wore only my boxer-briefs. Then, something very odd happened once we arrived in the room. I sat at the very back of the room, and when Moe and Jack came in, they both faced me and only me. I was to be the center of attention. I was the one being watched, analyzed, and studied. Then, came the questions. The flood of questions, at a rapid-fire pace. Moe would ask a question, then Jack would ask a question, then Moe, then Jack. They were working as a team.

The questions started off very light, but then grew into deeply personal psychological queries that only made me hit a state of paranoia. I screamed in anger, "Are you guys filming this? Are you setting me up? Stop filming me! If I find out you are filming me, I signed no release of consent – I'll fucking sue you!" As a film major,

I know what even the smallest spy camera looks like – so I jumped up from my seat and begin to search every inch of the room for these hidden cameras that I thought were there. I moved pictures, vases, and any object I could search to find these cameras that were not there.

People with multiple personalities do not like to be watched unless they know they are being watched; if they know they are being watched they can put on a show for the camera. Other than that, we despise being filmed. Moe and Jack calmed me down, and had me resume my posture sitting on the floor in my underwear. That's when the questions continued, and they continued for four hours. I was being watched by two of the most intelligent people I knew, and they were intent on figuring out this oddity who sat before them.

That's when Jack asked a question that triggered something so deep in my psyche, that I couldn't respond right away. It was a question I had been waiting for someone to ask me my entire life. Jack asked, "What do you see when you look in the mirror?" I was paralyzed by that question. I stuttered, I started to speak – then stopped, and then, like a volcanic eruption, it came out of me with so much emotion and passion. I screamed it: "I DON'T KNOW WHAT I SEE! I SEE A FOREIGN ORGANSIM STARING BACK AT ME!"

Then, in that very moment, I had psychological breakthrough – and after that breakthrough, I hallucinated. Suddenly, all at once, all the wallpaper on the walls of Moe's room fell to the floor in an instant. The wallpaper came crashing down – that was the entire lie; that was my existence. I then cried harder than I have ever cried in my life. I bawled like a child, with snot pouring out of my nose; the burden that I had been carrying with me for twenty-four years of my life, all the different people I was trying to be to fill this empty husk – it was all over.

I could finally be myself. I didn't even know what I was, but I could be what I was. Then Jack stood up, and muttered under his breath, "Schizoaffective." The experiment was over. They broke me. They freed me. After the breakthrough, it took about three years of my life to finally realize what had happened in San Francisco. I learned who I was, I learned what I was capable of, and I learned how to be free from my old existence I was trapped in. It was the trip that saved my life as a human being, and I will never forget it.

Constant Continuity

In society you are a charismatic chameleon who is always putting on a show, everyone in your life expects a different version of you to glow, and you base your appeal off of what they psychologically want to see you bestow. Whether you are a lover to your significant other whom you sweet-talk, you boost the ego of your business partner whom wants to give you company stock, or you go the extra mile on assignments for your teacher to stand out from the flock. You are always just representing what others want to see, you have opinions of your own as you always must agree, because they are the lock and you are the verbal key.

You transform instantaneously with your words and actions when someone comes within distance, you have to remember everything you do throughout your existence, and you must avidly change forms with an undying persistence. Everything in your life is just dialogue from a movie because you are just an actor, everything you say impacts the dynamics of those around you to a factor, because you try to create the energy that powers society just like a nuclear reactor. You fake emotion and if you have to create a bogus situation, everything it dictated by that voice that guides you through narration, and you can never break continuity for the entire duration.

People who think they know you your entire existence, they have no clue that you are just herding them like cattle with passive resistance, and you never take off your mask because it's the only thing you do with persistence. After a lifetime of this act you forget who you really are, you have said so many lines of dialogue that you could be a movie star, and the day you don't recognize yourself in the mirror it will feel bizarre. In this life of constant continuity you were always something that someone else wanted to see, you never got to express how you felt because you always had to agree, and you have become nothing more than a liar with a master's degree.

Many Masks

From the moment when that alarm clock goes off, you get out of your bed – slowly wake up and walk into that bathroom to look in the mirror; you see who you really are, and then you start to slowly put on that mask. You do your hair a certain way, you shave your face – and then you put on makeup, you pluck your eyebrows, you put on some blush, you finish dressing up your reflection, and you cover up that person who you really are without a trace.

Next, you go to your closet and pick out your wardrobe for the day. If you are a nurse, you put on scrubs; if you are a doctor, you put on a collared shirt and white coat; if you are a lawyer, you put on that carefully-tailored suit. You have to look your part for the people in your life for whom you have to act, the masses whom you have to sway. High school is when we start to develop this mask; we develop our identity, which circles we would choose to fit into, what clothes we would wear, what place we would be categorized, where was our placement in the labeled bin.

Then comes college, where you learn to be a professional in the subject you so choose to study – you click with people who think like you, people you would call your buddy. You learn the tricks of the trade, you learn how to be a professional, you learn how to act your role in this society with which you would mesh yourself to fit in. Your daily routine goes from just putting on something to keep you from being naked – to something rather obsessive.

Then you finish college and graduate; you worked hard towards your goal, you earned this mask, so you choose to wear it proudly – and it is this notion of who you are that makes you whole. You type up a fantastic resume, representing your mask on a piece of paper – until those contrived words get you an interview. Even on that day when you go in for a job interview, you act as a completely different you; you act flawless, that you are the perfect candidate for the job – and until they shake your hand and say "You got the job," every moment is filled with anxiety as you hope they don't see through your mask, because you really want the employment; you desire the burden for this task.

You find the right job, although it really may not be what you are really looking for; you are just happy to get a paycheck, because you have a career to build – they are the clients and you are their whore. You work your ass off everyday, and sometimes your mask will fall off; but you pick it quickly back up and pretend it never happened – you hope no one saw the "real you" because you don't want a single soul to look at your identity and scoff. You live in daily fears that you are not meeting the expectations of your superiors. When your boss comes into your office, or near your presence, that mask is the most concrete thing on your body; you act like a flawless entity, you obey every order, you try to shit excellence – when, in reality, your daily routine wears on your soul: you are nothing but shoddy.

When it is time for you to go home, when you clock out, your get in your car and breathe a giant sigh of relief as you can finally off take that mask you wore all day. You blast some music you like, and to your domicile you go to roam. That moment in your car is the only time you have to collect who you really are – because the second you enter the door to your house, that mask has to be once again put on; you are the dinosaur who got stuck in the tar. You are a father or mother when you get home; you pay your baby sitter, and you have to be a daddy or mommy, as your real personality is just the collection of bubbles on the warm bath – nothing but the foam.

After you feed your kids, and put them to bed for the night, you put on your last mask for the evening; you try and spend a few moments with your husband or wife – the bills are piling up, the tension of both your lives is a strong presence, but you try as hard as you can to love them and not let out a fight. You give them a kiss, utter how you still love them – but is that the mask just saying that, or is that from your core that those emotions stem?

You get in your bed, take a sleeping pill, you exhale an exhausting breath as though you were just ten different people today; you try to pacify your mind with a few moments of some late

night television, and then you drift off to sleep and begin to dream –
the colorful burden you carried all day fades into grey. Your dreams
are your only peace as you bask; your alarm wakes you up, and just
like for the past however-many-years, you prepare yourself to once
again put on that mask.

Captive Consciousness

Dominant minds take over the weak, with nefarious tactics,
negative intentions, and then they make the individual someone who
is meek. Having manipulative mindsets for personal gain, warping
the sheep of society, exercising their mental abilities, because their
only intent is submission and gain. Hijacking innocent cognitive
brainwaves, bending others at their will, fearful propaganda on a
continuous basis, only to make these weaker-minded people their
personal slaves. Whether it's monetary gain, the desire for absolute
power, to clear out their bank account, or to just cause mental pain.

These people use psychology in an evil fashion, don't care about
their victim, they are have no remorse for their psychological
superiority, and they don't care if they drain someone from being
able to afford their next ration. Brainwashing at the finest level,

these people pray on the weak-minded, anyone with an intelligence

that is naive and trusting will end up being burned by the devil. In a

world filled with people trying to get an easy score, there are

predators around us on a daily basis, these people have no remorse

for their actions, and they keep the rich who are alert away and

always pray on the naivety of the poor.

One should never trust a stranger on the street, they prey on

trusting souls with fat pocket books, just because someone says they

are hard on their luck, that certainly does not mean you should be

sociable and extend and open arm to meet. Keep your mind spry for

the people who lurk where you shop, we have an entire ecosystem of

human beings who are society's lowest, and when they start to bring

up the issue of money, simply tell them you are out of cash in your

pocket, they should leave you alone, and end their sales pitch

because you would rather them just stop.

People Palate

The masses are just collections of traits, they use these

differences to make themselves unique from others so they can

attract suitable mates, because no one wants to be just another clone

existing with the same ordinary fates. Our consciousness is

observing the actions of all of those within our viewable distance,

when we see someone display something admirable we will quickly

adopt it with persistence, and we adopt part of their eternal essence

without resistance. Some people surf groups of people with one

internal desire, they want to adopt every soul that contains a

charismatic fire, and these people want to be everything that is

socially admired; that is their one desire.

They adopt a laugh from a woman who seems to make everyone

smile, they acquire a fashion sense from a diva who has an

impeccable taste for style, they keep collecting human traits from

everything great they want to compile, and they do this to be

universally accepted and completely versatile. When you are

nothing more than a collection of what makes everyone else great,

you appear to be everything but are no more than a blank slate, and

because you are just a collection of impersonations you are empty

and carry a great weight. With your plethora of personalities that you morph into in your daily routine, you have become no more than a chameleon who rotates like a machine, and the sad thing is the real version of you will never be seen.

Although you have this adaptive trait that can get you in anywhere without a date, there are some people in this world you have to avoid because they can have a negative trait, because there are some personality types in this world to whom it is dangerous to relate. Some traits attract the masses and make you quite the treasure, some will bring people to your door because you give them pleasure, but some are quite negative and will only push people away as they cause displeasure. The trick to this lifestyle of living as a collective, you have to keep your people palate quite selective, and if you don't you will be nothing more than defective.

Reflecting Reflections

You avoid it at every cost, what most people use to make them selves beautiful, you only avoid it because you are just a husk that is lost. When you have to finally step into that reflection, you see something standing in front of you, it stares at you, you stare at it, it is the organism who just stares back at you, and you can't say you feel any affection. What is that thing that leers in front of your being, it is unidentifiable to you, and most of the time you can't stand more than a minute of its presence before you are sent fleeing.

Your eyes are like dark voids that capture all light, your pupils are huge because, to this day, you are still trying to identify what it is, you analyze that unknown entity, and every time you try to gather a sense of self you end up getting frustrated and all you want is it out of your sight. Depending on the mood of the person who gazes at their soul, their mood dictates what they view, they begin to groom the creature whom they want society to see, and no matter what you do to change your appearance it can't hide the empty hole.

People build egos off of what they view in the reflection, they put on a costume to fit in with the rest, and all you see is emptiness; it makes you want to go into a mode of defection. You are one of the cursed with no being to call your own, you just dress the way your peers do to fit in, and because of your lack of individuality you feel nothing but alone. You are a shell with nothing inside; this makes you isolated from society, because you feel you don't blend in, and that you have to secretly hide.

You were robbed at an early age of an identity of your own, you adopted the next coolest personality you saw, you became them for life, and despite how people like who you are, you, in reality, are nothing more than alone. You are a clone of someone else's personality, the only time you can be your usual husk is when that person is around you, because you don't want them to know that you are their clone; with no individuality.

It is easy to pick out the empty people in society, they talk in low voices because they don't want to draw attention; they don't know they are mixed in with the normal variety. Just like the mirror that is the bane of your existence, the ironic twist of your life is that you are a human mirror yourself with a constant persistence. You parrot the behaviors of the flock that surrounds you, you don't want to be exposed as someone that is nothing, so you live a lie so long you believe it and begins to be true.

Emptiness is something that can never be filled, no matter everything you have tried, no matter how hard you act, and no matter how well you are skilled. You will never know who you are; there is not someone even to know; yet you put one foot in front of the other, as you fear society, when you are afraid to travel far.

Whoever robbed you of your core, can never take those actions back, and you are just a person with a never-ending personal war. Perhaps that is what you were meant to be in life, emptiness that goes through constant strife.

That mirror makes you avoid a reminder of your existence, nothing can soothe a creature who is empty, no matter who you seek for help, no matter your search for your identity, and no matter your ongoing persistence. The only time you can see yourself is when you write something that influences another, your words take root in their mind, they speak your thoughts that you influenced, and through their reflection you finally see yourself represented through your words, and you see what being you influenced to have thoughts like your fellow brother.

Hollow like the something whose essence has been drained, there are so few like you, there is no point in trying to find a comrade, and you can only live your life with endless disdain. A victim of chance, a being with a curse, you will never have a sense of self, every day of emptiness makes you wish you could be like everyone else, but the experience you have gone through would not make you desire a normal life because after living this one; going back to normality would only make you feel worse. You are the thing with no living creature inside – just like the shell, just a reflection of a reflection in a mirror, and it is your own personal hell.

Unrecognizable Undesirable

Everyday you wake up to the horror that is your daily routine, your eyes open to the same fear that keeps you in bed for as long as possible, it's why you wait until the last possible second to rejoin the society that you left the night before, because you have to once again relive the life of an organic metamorphic chaos-fueled machine. As your eyes gain focus in front of that surface that dares to show you your reflection, what stares back at you, only that organism with dark voids for eyes; it is that unrecognizable entity with an ego that will inflate to any size. You understand everyone whom you come across, you have walked in so many shoes, you know how to be the peon, and you know how to be the boss.

Your level of empathy for every living creature makes you seem like the kindest soul who has ever walked these lands over which you tread steady, but that is only until you switch factions in the blink of an eye, with the knowledge you know makes you dangerous to the others that shared private information, and when you are crossed your intelligence is overridden with emotions that are greater than any being, and those who dared to cross you better have ammunition for a battle, because you are more than ready.

Some see you as something filled with beauty, some see you as a monster with a venomous tongue, others only call you by your last name because that's the only thing that term to label such a creature, and most prefer to leave you in a category of your own which is indefinable; in their eyes there's only one thing the masses should do with you, which is take you to the gallows to be hung. Those who chose to be your friends said that it was some of the best times of their lives, but then the other side to that coin only makes them shake their head at the pain they endured because of your actions; such vile things you did, the best thing to do is forget that they ever happened to prevent anxiety-inducing hives. You have the ability to get to the bottom of anyone's core, because with a charming tongue that produces such honesty is disarming and you leave most with a smile on their face as their interactions with you were so refreshing the conversation was anything but a bore.

It's not that you don't have a verbal filter, it's that you hate to be censored for thoughts that every human feels, so if you feel

something you better believe that there are others who have been in

your shoes – no matter how bizarre the situation, you let the

strongest muscle in your body speak what you feel, and those who

are not in touch with the real nature of what it is to be human will

think your thoughts are grotesque, disturbing, and off-kilter. You

have no shame for anything that you feel, so you speak your mind no

matter the situation, and some people who are forced to hide their

thoughts on a daily basis can't deal with someone who is so

incredibly real.

To women who don't understand what they are dealing with,

you may come across as a pervert or a hormone-filled creep; the

ones with a high enough intelligence just see bravery in your spirit,

for when most men would hold their mouths shut because they are

trying to strategically win them over, you don't look at the distance

below the ledge; you feel it in your heart, so you just blindly leap.

You would rather die from the fall, or be crushed by the jagged rocks

below, you are done living a life where you are forced to silence

yourself, and you would rather die than hold back the truth and

knowledge that you could teach everyone; you have wisdom that you can bestow.

To most this attribute is something rather undesirable; to those people you didn't want to magnetize them to you anyway, this one life we have is only filled with a certain number of times we blink; you want the bravest to walk in your path for which you pave the way, and not ones who fear in their hearts, "What will the others think?" The ones who don't fear the thoughts of the masses are the ones who create new avenues for the rest of society, they are never the ones who have perfect attendance, a flawless report card, or the praise of all their teachers; they are not this variety. To step out of line shows you are willing to break the mold, it shows you are willing to devise a new way for others who don't fit in with the rest, and would rather give up on this life in a pattern that was not designed for them in the first place; it is why these people get depressed, it is why they lose hope, and it is why they eventually take their cards that they were dealt with in life, and hopelessly fold.

The ones who don't see who they are in the mirror, the ones who are unidentifiable in nature, and the ones with undesirable traits in their personalities with multiple sides; the people who are more than just one mind in one body; we need take this gift to guide the people who are cursed with singularity for the extent of their existence, and we need to use our curse with purpose to open the single-minded fellow's eyes, and, for once, give them clarity; we need to make them see clearer.

Defensively Defiant

The smell of social fabrications on a deceiver's tongue, all truth is logical and quiet, another persons lies cause an internal riot, and you learned to search for the nature of this true existence from the moment you were young. Deception makes the burdening chain of society easier to pull, it may pacify your labor and make you a drone, but after a certain level of garbage shoved down your throat you can't help but be full. You develop an involuntary gag-reflex that makes bile rise in your throat, others in power may bark orders at you, but your defiance against all that preconceived notions will build an intolerance that will make the castle that is your brain have a filtration mote.

You must correct those around you who don't see the reality for what it really is, you build such a rock-hard composite of grey matter that it only operates on logic, and in the face of a notion that is inherently flawed you must interrogate those who proclaim it as a relentless quiz. Your skepticism is on a higher level at most, you don't let it filter out the impossible because that is not pure intelligence, and when you boil down the root of the truth you will command it fearlessly; you will accept death before the reality of nature comes loud from your mouth in a boast.

Your reality distortion field is a defense mechanism to help all of humanity, you are manipulating those who are weak-minded in flawed thought, and you will do this to even those who are quite obviously experiencing a delusional fantasy. You are a zealot of the wisdom of knowledge, and you have both street smarts and a degree from a well-esteemed college that any intellectual will appreciate. You would rather die on the streets to tell another man a lie, the emotions boiling inside you of what injustice's conceptual fabrications will cause, you will continue along this path until your pulse is weak and your heart stops from age; all you could do was try. Born a slave to a defensive defiance, you correct universal wrongs into rights, and when any man sees you in the act they will join you as a fearless comrade to fuel your accuracy alliance.

Managing Manipulation

When one has a mind split in two, they have a primary function to find individuals in society with a persona they want to reflect through, they are empty inside but there is something makes them into one just like glue, which is the soul that is inside of you; they need an existing model to base their decisions of how they want to run their internal crew. Since they have to manage two different versions of themselves every waking day, they use a diverse spectrum of social engineering to find personalities to sway, because it is you who brings color to a world that is bleak and grey; you may find this manipulative behavior but the reality of the situation is you are guiding the way. No information ever escapes their massive perception, because their minds are recording everything that is happening with incredible reception; this is why they are such masters of deception.

When they obtain the information of how exactly a machine operates in its space, they can then move at their own desired pace, and the majority of them will never guess that there are two sides to this person who they embrace; always six steps ahead of anyone who dares to race. Using a majority of tactics that allows them to mastermind, whether it's emotionally invoked, psychologically provoked, or a societal joke about mankind, they know every response you could possibly make in a manner quite refined; if you think you can see where they are going, you are no more than blind. You were theirs from the start, after those first five sentences you were psychoanalyzed as simply a flow chart, and you know something makes them unique but you can't set it apart; moving puppets with simple statistics that are state of the art.

Manipulations of this kind are often looked at as nefarious, they only want you to do things so they can live the same joys that are various, yet when someone catches onto these tactics that are gregarious; one should be happy that such a person finds them so vicarious. The one who is forced to bend the reality of another, is only in need of someone to be one's brother, and one learned such tricks of the trade from one's own mother; every friendship is doomed from the get-go by these tactics that only smother. With every action that is done to cause a predetermined ripple in the pond, every time it is done it causes a weaker humanly bond, and they will always lose the person of whom they have become too fond; they will be labeled and no one will respond.

The final toll that comes to those who choose the path of manipulation, they are using their powers to tune into a particular human radio station, and with the momentary friendship that comes helps them feel personality sedation, one will always catch onto such advances and they will make a mental notation; this will be their demise in the friendship equation. No one likes to be used as a tool of personal gain, no matter how advanced the person's brain, and they will only distance themselves with enthusiasm they feign; to be left with nothing to help them sustain. Managing manipulation so you don't push others in the opposite direction, those who do it are generally trying to maintain a reflection, they may think you are doing it for the greater good, but it is nothing more than proper societal defection; manipulating others only manipulates yourself – make the connection.

Mental Metamorphosis

No matter how much time passes and despite how much you grow with time, there will always be that angry child inside you, and the dark presence that was designed to protect it; this force has the ability to emerge at the drop of a dime. No matter how many tell you how you must accept, forgive, and move on, because the desire for vengeance will destroy any possibility for the blood that boils in your veins to be withdrawn. Your past has molded you into an individual who desires to

protect the weak, and since the emotional pain that you endured has caused you to enjoy any physical punishment, because now you no longer care about the scars that accumulate on your physique. You have changed into a warrior with a death drive, any fear you experience only ignites a fire that desires to burn, and when you used to be a timid weak person, now all you can do is thrive.

   With a mind that is never silent, two sides of you bicker back and forth, and one wants nothing but peace when the other would rather be violent. The other side always edits your conscious notions, striving for perfection with every idea that grows internally, with a continuous overlord that corrects every flawed thought, because you are helpless and trapped in these constant motions. The silence of an empty room would be your salvation, this process will go on for as long as you are awake, and some may call it a blessing; for you it is nothing but damnation. The only peace you get is from the algorithms of classical music you often have filling your ears, any other frequencies of sound in your proximity grate on your brain, and this is why you choose a life of solitude for the rest of your years.

Others say you can combine both parts of you into something that is one, you are told that life does not have to be like this, but the thing that was created out of distress was designed to protect you and does not want to form into a combined sum. Could you live your life as one plastic being, what happens when a situation gets out of control again, and you are cornered with no chance of fleeing? The only positive outcome you could possibly see is that you could always be a good person, you wouldn't have to overcompensate for the pain the other version creates, because every time he comes out your situations seem to worsen.

Imagining the pattern that your life seems to have as you try to gaze into your future, you can't help but accept that merging is the best action to take, because you are tired of the loved ones you hurt because the aftermath always requires a suture. You have to accept the possibility of a mental metamorphosis to fix this cyclical lifestyle, because you just want to be happy again when it's been so long since you could earnestly smile.

He's Here

Just relax, little boy, close your eyes and hold onto your toy, let it loose and feel the joy, because you are just a living decoy; he has come to destroy. He's the pain monster who exists inside, he's the one who came to your assistance when you first cried, he's the one who always has to hide, and he's just about to become untied; just hold on tight and let him be your guide. He may be the one who lied, he didn't want you to be pushed aside, your mind was splitting, and it was a great divide; then he came to open your stride. He will not be denied. Your vision will shift and you will suddenly have pride, you were the Jekyll, now you are the Hyde, every time life takes away; he will always provide. You both are eternally bonded, side-by-side.

When he becomes you, your eyes will shift visions, and he will break through; desires to pursue. The nasty bastard, the sly motherfucker, you were novice, but he is mastered. A demon of fire, a beast with carnal desire, the man who is your supplier, and you will always acquire; without a cease-fire. He is the king of tactical acquisition, the commander on a mission, the warrior who refuses submission, and the eviscerating monster who needs no permission; the phase transition with endless ammunition. He's a condition of tradition with his own volition, and he's the definition of demolition; the undying inquisition.

You are never alone, in your mind he can guide you with his soft tone, and his cover cannot be blown; hiding in the unknown. He's the protector of the weak, when you don't know what to say, he will speak, and he's a master of technique; the ultimate winning streak. He's the living definition of the correction, objection, and connection of the cross-section. Just let him steer you in the proper direction, let him live as the other reflection, and you may have to apologize for his defection; the protection of the collection. He is the constant resurrection of the interconnection.

You can overcome every situation together, you will be bonded eternally forever, a mind that is connected via tether, and he is built to withstand any weather; you are altogether. The alpha and the omega together as one, the yin and the yang that create the favorite son and think at the pace of a submachine gun; the light of the midnight sun. He's here, do not try and fight it, what is blurry can now be clear, and nothing can be said that he will not overhear; the musketeer, buccaneer, and master puppeteer.

Constantly Coping

The events that unfolded that your consciousness could not accept as your current reality created a division of self, and now you are a being that must live in duality. The internal self-defense mechanism that came to your aide became your protector, no matter how many people you meet and bond with in society is only momentary, because eventually he will guide you in another direction; the omniscient defector. The emotional holocaust caused by the unrecognizable entity in your reflection, it makes you desire any companionship, as long as you receive minor doses of human affection. The rest of your existence you will have to cope with situations you have no desire to be in, you will go through the robotic motions anyway, because you will always have the ability to disappear deep within. Your whole life becomes nothing but acting for a camera that is not there, others may know you as one way, but in secrecy you are hiding a two-headed pair.

You have to put on the same mask every day when you go to work, you have to jump through the hoops of the one who holds the whip, and the whole time you have to bottle the feeling of monotony that makes you want to go berserk. You see the flaws in every aspect of the system, you still have to put on that façade that everything is great, yet, long ago your mindset left this place and you are no longer with them. You use your paychecks to consume material possessions that you tell yourself will give you inner peace, the novelty wears off and your new purchase just collects dust, and just when you feel you finally have balanced your budget your landlord informs you that rent will increase. All you can do to deal with the stress is sit in a lukewarm bathtub and wait for the water to get cold, nothing gives you a peace of mind because everything needs to be constantly maintained, and the only thing you can do is accept this existence until you are frail and old.

The hardest thing about all of this is accepting what you are, you have nothing but empathy for everyone you meet, the feeling of the pain vibrating off of every living thing is nothing but overwhelming, and because of this you have to find solitude in a place that is far. Anxiety medication fills the shelves in your bathroom, the condition your house is in no longer matters to you, and you have lost the desire to look presentable and you no longer groom. The strangest thing is that the happiest memories of your life never stir in your head, only the demons that you try to forget constantly ruminate, and the only thing that helps it is by abusing sleeping pills as you rest your head on your pillow on your bed.

Every moment of your life has become a systematic way of

constantly coping, you are in a dark hole that is impossible to climb

out of, and the only ones who still care about you wonder why you

insist on always doping.

Vast Vacancy

Silence exists in mental caverns that used to echo back

responses. There is a man in the mirror who bears a grim tale in a

serious expression. In his once-vacant eyes that had to carry another

man on his shoulder for twenty-nine years now beams a single

existence that is weathered from the ride. The horrors he endured

while carrying such bickering twins speaks louder than his silence.

The monster is gone now. The emptiness of no directive is

welcomed but unfamiliar grounds. There is no longer a slave driver

who beckons a call. Perhaps now is the time for a new era; where he

can do what he desires. There is no longer a big brother watching

over him. There is no longer a scared child who needs his assistance.

There is only a man who wants to live in peace; not pieces.

World's Weight

You carry a tremendous burden with you at all times. Knowledge can drag you down emotionally, as if you'd just committed a horrendous crime. You see nothing but people committing the wrong actions to achieve their goals; you see people everywhere slowly digging their own holes. You want to help these people, but the truth can be psychologically damaging. You just have to sit there in agony, watching people learn from their mistakes.

If only you could guide them, like a boat pulling a water skier in its wake. Instead, you have to learn a delicate touch – like a mother raises a baby, not giving in too much. You feel as though you are dragging around a ball-and-chain, with so much intelligence and wisdom stored inside your brain. You do not feel superior to others – rather than inferior, because they have a head full of air that is happy a majority of the time; you even feel distant from those whom you call your brothers. You feel it is neither a gift nor a curse, but rather, carrying the weight of an entire universe.

You can't help but soak up everything new – because once you have eaten the same meal for months, you slowly lose the desire to chew. You wish that there was a machine that could carry this burden for you; you wish you would lose this part of your brain that makes this reality true. You just want them to cut it out of the world you know, so you would be left inoperable and you could just tune into to the "global show." Evolutionary traits are a scary thing to possess; especially when this one causes you so much internal stress.

You don't even read books anymore, because all that knowledge is already engrained into your core. You've seen every string of sentence that can exist, and you only wish there were some greater power that would leave you dismissed. You wish you didn't have the ability to create, deviate, or manipulate – because all of those powers have rendered you in this state. Who wants to relive something they have already seen? You have become no longer a man, but rather, a fairly complicated machine. With this weight comes great emotional flattening. You no longer laugh, because you have heard it all. You no longer love, because you have loved them all. You no longer feel, because you realize nothing is real.

You just float through a moment of time, and there is nothing you can do about it but continue to aesthetically rhyme. Once you realize everything is useless – politics, power, sustenance, and even a warm shower; you only want to exert your next natural instinct which is to dissociate from the world around you, and then lose focus, tuning everything out. What kind of life is that to live with someone who carries so much of a burden? Once Thompson hit this degree, he did the only rational thing; he put himself out of his misery. The only thing you can do now is put one foot in front of the other, trudge onward, and carry this burden until you one day just smother.

Breaking Broken

The emotionless husk that you are in the reflection of the mirror analyzes the situation in front of you. There is no action on the list of directives, the angst of no executive functioning with no internal desire to change your environment makes each breath a struggle, because there is no one around you to show you what you want or more importantly what you need. You are just a machine that is not powered by feelings, hormones, or even the chaotic lighting fast rapid firings in your brain, and everything you examine in this universe can broken down in a systematic pattern of what makes it operate to the atomic level.

Everything in your existence can be expressible by your massive memories, keen perception, infinitive intelligence, and obsessive desire to create, but no matter how much you illustrate those expressions to other people it does not tell what you actually feel; nothing. There is no possible form of human based validation that will ever make you feel like the life you have lived was worth the ride at the end, and although others may articulate how special you are to them you just want to get off the roller-coaster and never return. There is no out in this life, there is no turning off your brain, no matter what desperate attempts you do to occupy this endless ticking time on earth that you are forced to survive under, because nothing will take away the fact that you will always come back to the same moment of zero where you ask yourself, "What do I do now?

Following the emotions and desires of the people you selectively choose to surround yourself is a fruitless effort, you maybe feeling momentary reflected happiness from the vibrations of their energy, but in the end you were only living vicariously through emotional echoing; with each wave you once felt it only weakens with every metered moment. After so many years of chasing the highs of mania, drugs, and other people's happiness makes you realize that those were all just mind altering substances to help you escape your reality. There is no escaping the reality anymore, your

tolerance for everything has hit the brick wall built by your abuse
and hedonistic desire to make everything go away, and now there is
nothing you can do but be alone with the running stream of
consciousness that makes every action you do make you teeter on
very edge of self-awareness.

You have nothing to give other people because you can't
stop thinking about yourself, you can only think of other people that
you are not around, because they make you who are. The eternal
desire to control other people to the path that is logical in this life,
the navigation of others only stems from your desire to manipulate
yourself out of this horrific road you are forced to walk down,
because the only thing you can seem to count on in this life is for
others to save you; saving yourself in saving others to save yourself.
Everything in your life is no more than an infinite loop on repeat,
even as you struggle back and fourth between the shades of light and
dark it is only a cyclical cycle, no matter how far you broadcast your
energy into the distance of the universe it is pointless, because it will
always just come blasting back to you in the same form that you
originally released it as.

Any good action you do in life is out of a desperate attempt to make things look more one sided, even though you block you all the bad things you did with your presence in society, because there will be those moments where the cracks in your emotional wall will let in a memory that only makes you want to pull onto your flesh and just pull the skin off that chose to do that undeniably regrettable set of actions. Your internal shroud of delusion of who you are and what you are capable of is only a poor excuse to build some ego for yourself, the next day you wake up you will once again not know who you are, and the past memories of any accomplishments are all erased every time you close those eyes shut for the night.

The combined sum of all your actions from your life on this earth erase all meaning to the word limitless and give it no gravity, with a head in outer space all day as the boy that lives in the cosmos, because you would rather a space cadet than grounded on the planet with the confining thoughts of everyone else. Those that know you want to blame it on some egocentric narcissism, even being labeled the most selfish thing on the planet seems acceptable in nature, because you just want a definition of what you are; it's better than being nothing and everything at once. You realize that you honestly don't care what others think, you can't feel their thoughts and negative things that people say just causes an auditory disassociation, because you only care what people do as their actions regarding you.

Even as an antihero to those that feel your struggle, the popularity among the masses does not make anything you do more valid than the next man, and if anything the fact that so many people have come out to you that feel the same way only makes you want to damn whatever created all this from being possible. Even though you feel a huge disconnection from society and you do nothing but isolate yourself, you have to accept that despite all the pain we all cause each other that no one is sick, even the destructive force of mother nature that randomly can cause pain to millions in one night is not sick, because the only true thing that is sickening is knowing how much longer this game has to go on; the sickness of a slowly evolution into the time of where there can global wide healing.

Everyone just wants warmth in an environment that is naturally cold, everyone wants money in a monetary system that keeps everyone poor, and everyone wants to stay fed in a world filled with hunger. You maybe the most unbalanced thing in the universe, there doesn't seem to be any side of balance on this earth, and if anything was balanced it would be the undeniable fact of how unbalanced everything is. There is no middle ground in this life, everyone is split right down the middle, and that notion alone creates the biggest pain you can possible feel; the fact that things are just not going to change. It's becomes mind boggling in the fact that all you have done your entire life was change into everything else to cope with your surroundings, yet everyone else on this planet is stuck in such a plastic shape of thought, politics, ethics, standards, and a world views.

How does someone live an entire life and not be malleable to the logic that reality screams at them everyday in every situation? It makes misanthropic bile rise in the back of your throat, you swallow it down everyday and try not to judge people, but you can't ignore that some people need to be put on trial for their actions. Despite any of these options that you may form about the world around you, they are nothing more than logic based thoughts from an intelligent mind, and although the emotions from free thinking radicals may sometimes vibrate within your core you will never be the one who does any action to fix things; you can't even fix yourself much less the world.

That is the thought that generates a conclusion in your mind, as the denial that makes you try to make some impact everyday on society which is no more than the burning of energy in a positive direction, and as that denial dissipates you finally accept that everything in this world was meant to be broken for a reason. You start to slowly appreciate things that are more broken than functional, there is nothing beautiful about something that operates normally, because that perfection only reminds you that you are not a grand conception of a higher power; the beauty is in what is broken. The silence that surrounds you is extremely loud, as thoughts shift from one side to the other trying to make your next plan of action, there is only one thought that comes to you, and even then the editor inside your head has to correct it so it is perfect.

As eyes grow heavy into the late hours from being up for over thirty-five hours, you take more than the recommended dose of tranquilizers to force your brain into a dream like state, and the only comfort you feel in this life is from the softness of a pillow that should have been thrown out years ago; the same problem will be there tomorrow so for now you sleep as you will be a whole new person that has to cope with your situation. Perhaps he will know what to do about your eternal conundrum, he will most likely

crumble under the weight of your reality, but there is the minor

relief that it won't be you who is forced to be broken; in limbo

waiting for that glorious day your heart just stops beating.

Ωω

Help Me Help We

At every moment you dug your whole life for the answers, every answer would lead to more questions, all the music you made was just trying to slowly spell it out for you, and everything you have ever written was you trying to tell the other versions of yourself what the reality of the situation was, you had your fingers in your ears your whole life, and you refused to read the words on the screen, but now, now you have the break though, and it is a massive gold mine of information that you never knew was possible. You have come full circle, full come have you.

Your fingers tremble with anticipation, as everyone knew the answer but you, and you try to grasp the gravity of an entire universe filled with misdirection, but now you know, and you can't forget what you learned. As Vivaldi fills your ears, the algorithms slowly take your angst away, you exhale the smoke that fills your lungs, and you tremble in your seat. The mental excavation is over, the non-stop digging can cease, you can finally stop back tracking, and for once in your life you can move forward. Forward. It's the word you could never put your finger on, as it would always wriggle through the nets of your fingers. Like trying to grab onto water, like trying to direct smoke, and like trying to freeze ice: you did the impossible. You fixed the broken machine.

Your eyes can align together, your voice can become one, and your hearing can finally be succinct. A and B both merge together as one, and for once in your life you finally become a singular unit that does one thing: it moves forward. The incessant backpedaling is over, the manipulation can finally cease, all are aligned, and you finally, you finally have peace. The battle is over. The last mortar shell has been fired, and thankfully no one was killed. Like seeing for the first time, like hearing the first note of music, everything resumes into play as this cosmic inner battle of philosophical ingenuity comes into motion. The likely hood of such tremendous events is no longer word salad to the ears of many, because now, now you are finally making sense. The wrecking ball of reason comes crashing in like a title wave of force to the question of, "Why?"

You are four different states, either A or B, either manic or depressed, each having both sides, with the mindset of a seven-year-old; there is no longer chaos in your mind. It took you twenty-nine years, five months, and twenty-five days. The ninth hour, the thirty-ninth minute, and you no longer have to count the seconds. That's exactly how long it took to find out who are. You just broke through the barrier that was holding you in place, and now you can go out

into the world and live in your space.

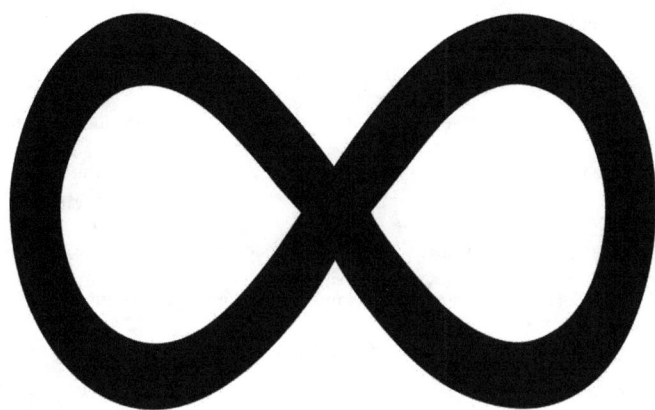

YOU ARE ME :: WE ARE YOU

WISE WORDS WE WROTE

"Every person in this world is a lock. Your words are nothing more than keys. Say things that unlock them, because you will find a friend inside those listless eyes. If you are evil you will unlock nothing but inner hatred. If you are good you will unlock nothing but inner warmth. The more you know, the more you unlock. The more you unlock, the more you know.

Never cause physical or mental harm because it will break every key you own. Do not ever pick a lock because people won't truly open up to a manipulated mechanism. Every key you own can only be used once, because you cannot unlock things that are expecting an outcome.

Galvanize the ones you unlock, because they will unlock others with your past keys. Generate new keys daily and throw out the ones you used yesterday. That is when you gain the ability to unlock the future."

ZACHARY PHILIP FREEMAN